Steven Jay Urry
A Retrospective

May 10 – July 19, 2012

Koehnline Museum of Art

Oakton Community College

Exhibition curators: Victor M. Cassidy and Nathan Harpaz

Catalog by Victor M. Cassidy

FOREWORD

The exhibition *Steven Jay Urry: A Retrospective* at the Koehnline Museum of Art is another milestone in the Museum's mission to promote regional artists and enhance its sculpture program.

In 1999, the College dramatically expanded its sculpture parks at the Des Plaines and Skokie campuses through a long-term loan program initiated when seven large-scale works moved to Oakton from Pier Walk, Navy Pier's annual outdoor sculpture show. Since that time, both sculpture parks have continued to grow and now feature more than 50 sculptures. In 2007 and 2010, the Museum also produced two major *Sculpture Invasion* exhibitions in partnership with Chicago Sculpture International.

In his book *Fantastic Images: Chicago Art Since 1945*, published in 1972, Franz Schulze described Steve Urry's sculptures in poetic terms, noting, "There is a heavy muscularity to his rambling aluminum blooms and big color gobbets, and even a winking wit which seems to derive from comic strip sources." This retrospective revisits the short but brilliant career of this forgotten artist, who reached the pinnacle of his profession in Chicago during the late 1960s and 1970s.

Several Chicago artists who knew Urry during his time in Chicago are linked to the Koehnline Museum of Art. In 1981, Marvin Jumes, M.D., and his wife donated Richard Hunt's bronze *Serpentine Winged* to the College, and in 2001 the Museum produced the exhibition *Richard Hunt: Wings*. The Museum acquired Jerry Peart's painted aluminum sculpture *Hoop La La* through an Illinois Arts Council grant in 1982, and followed that up with the exhibition *Alpha and Omega: Small Sculptures and Models by Jerry Peart* in 2003. In 2005, John Adduci's sculpture *Armillary* was installed at the Art, Science, and Technology Pavilion in the Skokie campus as part of the Illinois Percent for Art Program. In this catalog, Hunt, Peart, and Adduci recount their inspiring encounters with Urry.

I would like to thank the private collectors and museums that generously lent works or permitted the use of images for this exhibition. I would like also to acknowledge the exhibition's curator, Victor Cassidy, for his extensive work researching and writing this catalog, the most complete documentation and evaluation of Urry's life and work ever produced.

Nathan Harpaz, Ph.D.
Manager and Curator
Koehnline Museum of Art

The art world has yet to acknowledge Steve Urry's sculpture. Dead for less than 20 years, he is all but forgotten except by the artists who knew him. A few museums own Urry's sculptures, but most of his surviving work remains in private hands. Much is lost.

Many artists seemingly vanish after their deaths. What justifies a special interest in Steve Urry? Why organize a retrospective exhibition and write a catalog?

Urry (1939-1993)brought metal to life and made it plastic. Unlike earlier metal sculptors whose work embodied industrial and architectural forms, Urry created exuberant, often humorous aluminum sculptures that suggest trees, flowers, buds, clouds, and other natural forms. He imagined form in three dimensions and could conceive of how objects were placed in three-dimensional space. He opened fresh territory for art by exploring biomorphic form and sculptural space as no other sculptor had done before him. What he dreamed he built.

Urry clarified his ideas by drawing and then spent laborious hours welding, grinding, and polishing his sculptures. Often he cast or ground smaller elements and assembled them into larger pieces to create work with an improvisational character. Late in his career, he sawed metal sculptures from aluminum billet in a single session. Like all the best artists, Urry rarely repeated himself. He sought the new as he experimented with form, scale, and material.

Born into a professional Chicago family, Steve Urry discovered art in late adolescence, started out to be a painter, and found his way to sculpture while he was an art student in San Francisco. For two years after leaving school, he developed his work as he lived in a San Francisco building full of artists. Decisive influences were the West Coast sculptors Robert Hudson and Alvin Light, who sought to translate Abstract Expressionism into three dimensions.

In 1964, Urry returned to Chicago, where he made large-scale San Francisco-influenced sculptures from steel until a local arts patron gave him all the aluminum he wanted—for free. After that, he worked large-scale in aluminum, and success followed astonishingly fast. He showed solo in a local gallery in 1966. A year later, he had a one-man show in New York. Then, in 1969, he became the first local artist to have a solo exhibition at Chicago's Museum of Contemporary Art.

Chicago was an ideal environment. Urry had a huge studio and made friends among local artists who had organized to seek recognition for their work. He joined Chicago's close, supportive sculptural community whose leaders created a market for large-scale outdoor sculpture. Viewed by most as a San Francisco product, Urry acknowledged some influence from Chicago's Imagist painters and their impudent, cartoonish work.

Urry made pedestal sculptures in the early 1970s, experimenting with scale, materials, ways of building up, surface, and fabrication. He concentrated his forms, and his work became more subtle and intimate. At this time, he participated in important group exhibitions, completed several commissions, and sold his sculpture through Chicago and New York galleries.

Hoping for national recognition, Urry moved to New York City in 1973. By this time, he had begun experimenting with plastic as a material for sculpture. Starting with transparent vinyl, he moved on to polyurethane isocyanate resin, making large-scale sculptures of intestinal and biomorphic forms. He exhibited these sculptures solo in two Michigan museums during 1976-77, but the work was destroyed on its return journey to New York. Urry and his career never recovered from this devastating loss. After 1977, he had no dealer and was in no important shows. His public career had lasted just 11 years.

Urry departed New York in 1981 and spent the rest of that decade assisting other sculptors in Miami and Chicago. During this time, he built small aluminum and polystyrene sculptures, and made abstract paintings. His 1980s work became less complex and more intuitive. In 1993, the year of his death, Urry was 54 years old and living with his retired parents in Tempe, Arizona.

Artists who acknowledge Urry's influence include the sculptors Jerry Peart and John Adduci, who worked with him in Chicago. John Henry has said that Urry's uncompromising determination to build what he saw in his mind inspired him at an early stage in his career.

Steve Urry lived for his sculpture. Though making art was the most important thing in his life, personal feelings are not discernible in his work. He thought visually, worked intuitively, and put his ideas into his art. Never very articulate or knowledgeable about art, he talked shop with colleagues and was more of a presence than a teacher on occasional forays into the classroom.

Tall and lanky, Urry was a good-looking man who dressed cowboy style and charmed many people, women especially. Colleagues testify that he was an inspiring sight in the studio. He delighted in his work, had excellent making skills, and, once started, only stopped when exhausted.

Urry was no financier, but he did earn money from his work. Through most of his public career, he had New York and Chicago gallery representation, and he sold some work privately. He successfully applied for commissions, awards, and group shows. Even with all this, he never penetrated New York. All his major shows were in the Midwest.

Indifferent to money, Urry was never fully self-supporting for more than short periods in his life. He let others take care of him so that he could work in his studio. Subsidized by his parents, he took art classes for seven years in four different schools, never earned a degree, and accepted their support during the four-year apprenticeship that followed. He loved his indulgent mother and faithful sisters. Other women provided sexual companionship, housekeeping, and child care. His best friends were men and he was closer to his brother Lynn than to anyone else.

Acknowledgments

Nathan Harpaz, manager and curator of the Koehnline Art Museum at Oakton Community College, consented to this retrospective exhibition, providing funding for it as well as much valuable guidance with this catalog, which was designed by Nancy Nash Sidlin. Dan Blue funded the show installation which was designed by Ron Gard.

This is the first extended treatment of Steve Urry's life and work. When he died, Steve left sculptures, press clippings, business letters, photographs of his work, and a two-page résumé. These materials led me to many of Steve's contemporaries who answered my questions and suggested the names of other informants—and helped me find his sculptures. Many of the photographs were untitled and undated, but informants helped me make sense of them and construct a career narrative.

The prime movers of this enterprise are Steve's siblings—Lynn, Kay, and Janis Urry—who answered a thousand questions and loaned photographs and artwork in their possession. John Adduci, the Chicago sculptor who housed Steve in his home and studio at different times in the 1980s, provided much technical support to a writer who is ignorant of metals fabrication. He also answered many questions as he housed and restored the sculptures in the retrospective exhibition.

Many thanks to Dennis Adrian, Mary Baber, Dave Beck, Lindy Bergman, Robert Bergman, Peter Bradshaw, Brian Boyer, Ron Davis, Kim Del Giorno, Elaine Smith Dunlap, Larry Edwards, Ted Garner, Gail Gesteihr, Barbara and Erwin Glass, Carl Gliko, Steve Grenier, Jeff Gunderson, Michael Hall, Peter Holbrook, Robert Hudson, Richard Hunt, Mavis Jukes, Terrence Karpowicz, Mary Ann Keeler, Larry Kornegay, Linda Kramer, Ellen Lanyon, Art Martin, Ron Nagle, Dawn Clark Netsch, Kathy Paddor, Jerry Peart, Pamela Popeil, Claire Prussian, Richard Rosenzweig, Tom Scarff, Franz Schulze, "Tassy," Dolores Thurlby (AKA "Sprite"), Susan Varick, Carlos Villa, and James Zanzi.

I also thank Billy Bengston, Peggy Boutin, Paul Clark, Jordan Davies, Stan Edwards, John Henry, Rodger Jacobson, Joshua Kind, Vaughan Kurtz, Karen Lennox, James Melchert, Ron Nagle, Don Seiden, Caleb Urry, and David Wolf. Special thanks to Christia Blankenship, Janice Dillard, and "Jude" of Chicago's Museum of Contemporary Art, the staff at the Burnham Library, the Art Institute of Chicago, and to Barbara Gilbert, University of Chicago Library, Department of Special Collections.

Wherever possible, the author credits professionals who photographed Steve's work. Some of the photographs in this book had no name on the back. Whenever they did, the author made a conscientious effort to locate the photographer. Not all citations are complete in the Documentation section of this catalog. The author did the best he could, given limitations of time and funding.

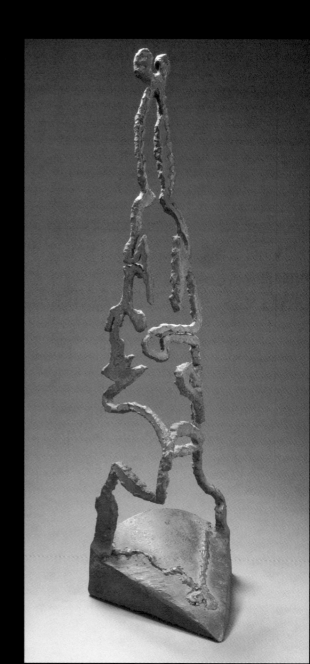

Steven Jay Urry was born on September 5, 1939, in Chicago, Illinois and grew up in a professional-class family near the University of Chicago. His father Wilbert Herbert Urry, earned a doctorate in chemistry (1946) from the University of Chicago and then rose through the ranks there, serving as professor of chemistry from 1957 until his retirement in 1980. Known to friends and colleagues as Bill (he hated the name "Wilbert"), Professor Urry published 76 professional papers; served as consultant to the Army, Navy, and private industry; won important academic honors; and served on boards of scientific societies. Steve inherited his father's investigative, experimenting temperament, but applied it to art and art-making.

Some have confused Bill Urry with Harold Clayton Urey (1893-1981), the physical chemist who received the Nobel Prize in 1934 for his pioneering work on isotopes. Harold Urey taught at the University of Chicago, but he and Bill were not related. Their names are spelled differently. From time to time, the Urrys and the Ureys socialized.[2]

The Urry family came from Salt Lake City, Utah, where Bill was born in 1914, eldest of a Mormon bishop's nine children. Many of Bill's siblings practiced the Mormon faith, but he and his children did not. Mormon missionaries always seemed to find the Chicago family.

Bill married Dion Brown on November 6, 1936. Her father was an itinerant who showed movies in small Idaho towns and sometimes received payment in chickens. Dion, a very attractive woman, never completed high school but was known in the university community as a gracious hostess and a very good listener. She devoted herself to her four children: Lynn, Steven, Kay, and Janis.[3] She handled the family finances, always treating Steve generously. More open to Mormonism than her husband, she encouraged her children to attend church but without success.

Bill put all that he had into his work and was distant from his family. When he came home from the university, Dion shushed the children and dinner was eaten in silence. After his retirement, Bill worked as a consultant for two or three years, but a massive stroke on a consulting trip left him unable to speak. Bill and Dion remained in the Hyde Park home until late 1984 or early 1985, eventually moving to Tempe, Arizona. In his final years, Bill became more responsive to his sons and daughters, but by then they were grown.

Said to be "very shy and kind" as a child,[4] Steve became a typical teenager who joined the high school swim team and liked to hang out with friends. His sweetheart in Hyde Park High School was Gail Schwartz, the daughter of a Chicago lawyer. Steve and Gail joined a motorcycle club, went to races, and had a lot of fun. According to his brother Lynn, Steve owned a 650cc Triumph—a stock street machine—and Lynn had a 500cc Matchless. Steve learned basic cycle mechanics at this time and some of his sculptural forms recall motorcycle parts.

A Year in Berkeley

Bill spent the year 1957-58 as an exchange professor of chemistry at the University of California–Berkeley, taking the family with him. The Urrys drove to California, stopping off to visit relatives in Salt Lake City. While there, Steve drew portraits at family gatherings. According to his sister Kay, Steve "just had an ability to draw these portraits [of] family members in Salt Lake, all these Mormons who were sitting around." Steve's drawings were well received and Kay thinks that this "was the first acknowledgment that he ever got from anybody that he had a talent in anything. It kind of took off from there."

Steve loved California—it was cool. He took auto shop and welding at Berkeley High School. According to Lynn, he built a ramshackle hot rod body from scrap metal, using an acetylene torch and coat hangers for welding rod. Gail says that he learned how to modify his motorcycle in Berkeley.[5] When Steve returned to Chicago from California, Lynn, who had stayed behind for his freshman year at the University of Chicago, remembers that Steve's Triumph "no longer looked like a Triumph. . . Steve [had] . . . bored the cylinders out as far as he dared . . . put lightweight racing pistons in it so it could reach higher rpm without blowing up . . . increased the compression ratio . . . replaced the smaller stock intake valves with bigger Ford tractor valves . . . [and] installed bigger carburetors."

Steve's chopper had become a speed machine, a café racer, and there was talk of a race against a school friend who had, as Lynn remembers it, a "Vincent black shadow . . . an incredible lightweight 1000cc machine" that was "fast, black, and evil-looking." Maybe the race took place, maybe not—no one knows. What matters is that Steve had his first experiences with metals fabrication in California.

While Steve was living in Berkeley, Gail flew to San Francisco and told him that she was pregnant. They married in October of 1958 in Chicago's City Hall and stayed in the city. Gail's first pregnancy ended in a miscarriage, but she gave birth to a daughter, Kim, on June 1, 1959. The Jewish Schwartz family was not pleased with Gail's gentile husband, but they and Dion Urry helped raise Kim and always treated her with affection. Kim remembers that Bill Urry once took her outdoors and showed her the constellations in the night sky.[6]

Steve and Gail had an apartment near 71st Street, which was approximately a mile south of the Hyde Park neighborhood. He was employed at the Griswold & Bateman Warehouse, but the experience soured him on factory work and his siblings speculate that he may have decided to pursue art at this time. He studied watercolor and drew scenes of Lake Michigan and the Gothic-style architecture on the University of Chicago campus. Kim has a watercolor drawing he did then, which is apparently the only one to survive.[7]

Two high school friends—Bob Silverman and Paul Butterfield—introduced Steve to Chicago's bars and night life. Gail recalls "a bar we hung out at in Hyde Park with Bob Silverman. It was more folk music than blues [with] peanut shells on the floor." According to his sister Janis, Steve "loved clubs and went a lot." At Pepper's Lounge and the Blue Flame, he heard blues musicians like Jimmy Reed, Muddy Waters, and Little Walter. Butterfield (d. 1987), who played the harmonica with the bands and sang the blues, drank beer "all the time," says Janis, and "got into drugs."[8]

First Art Training

Steve received his first formal art instruction in Chicago. He states in his résumé that he took classes at the University of Chicago and the School of the Art Institute of Chicago between 1957 and 1959. Neither institution has any record of him, which suggests that he went at night and on weekends but did not register as a degree candidate.

By 1960, Steve and Gail had returned to San Francisco, and he was taking classes at the California College of Arts and Crafts. Steve worked as a night watchman, and the couple lived in a brownstone where heat came up through a grate in the center of the floor. They put a barrier around this grate so Kim would not hurt herself by crawling across it.[9] Two oil paintings, measuring 23 x 33 in. and dated 1960, have survived: a semi-abstract *Folksinger* and an abstract pattern piece titled *Detachment*. Both were offered at auction in 2002, failed to sell, and remain untraced.[10]

The Urry-Schwartz marriage disintegrated in San Francisco. When Gail was diagnosed with leukemia, she took her baby and went to Chicago for a second opinion. That diagnosis indicated that she was merely anemic. Instead of returning to

San Francisco, Gail divorced Steve. Kim was three years old when she saw Steve for the last time. He made her a chain of rubber bands. In following years, he sent her one or two small gifts, but that was all she got from him until much later in his life when they talked on the telephone.[11]

The California College of Arts and Crafts has no record of Steve's attendance in 1960-61, but Tassy,[12] the woman who met him there and who became his second wife, confirms his attendance. Now called the California College of the Arts, this institution offered instruction in painting, drawing, sculpture, printmaking, and design.[13] Tassy recalls that a "Robert Stern" (Not listed in the 1960-61 CCAC Catalog: possibly Eric E. Stearne, Associate Professor of Design) influenced Steve in design and composition. She adds that he took a sculpture class.[14]

The California College of Arts and Crafts emphasized training in design ahead of fine art. Steve, who wanted to be a fine artist, transferred in 1961 to the San Francisco Art Institute (SFAI), whose program and faculty could better meet his needs. Attendance and grade records from the SFAI—the only documentation we have of Steve's post-secondary education—show that he took drawing and color, sculpture, and metal sculpture in the 1961 fall semester, and painting/studio and Eastern art history in the 1962 spring semester.[15]

Among Steve's teachers at the SFAI, the most influential seems to have been David Tolerton, a monumental sculptor who had been a blacksmith and worked in iron and steel. According to Carlos Villa, an Abstract Expressionist painter who graduated from SFAI in 1961, Tolerton was a "terrific teacher" who brought blacksmith tools into the welding shop and trained Robert Hudson and Rodger Jacobsen, two major San Francisco artists.[16]

Tassy, the daughter of a Bay Area lawyer, was just 18 when she married Steve on August 1, 1961. She transferred with him to the SFAI, and they lived in an Oakland duplex. There, Steve set up his studio in the garage, where he built stretcher frames—big for him, smaller for her. "He did abstract painting," Tassy recalls, "and made his own paint, some of which I used also. He painted very large canvases and painted all night when he was inspired . . . His [paintings] were quite large (floor to ceiling and I remember one would cover a living room wall)."[17]

Tassy adds that during their marriage, Steve "really started concentrating on soldering and welding sculptures. He really liked working with the torch. He was really influenced by James Dean, rebel without a cause. However, Steve wasn't all that noble (he would probably say so too)."[18]

Three Early Sculptures

Three sculptures that Steve cut from steel sheet and welded together in 1961 and 1962 have survived, and Tassy was able to date two of them. *Untitled* (Gift to Father) and *Untitled* (Gift to Mother) were presented to Steve's parents "not long after we were married [in August of 1961] or just before we were married," Tassy writes. "I saw those at his father's house [in Chicago after February of 1962] when . . . our child was a baby." *Untitled* (Gift to Lynn), which Steve gave to his brother around 1970 is stylistically similar to the other two and was presumably made at about the same time."[19]

Untitled (Gift to Lynn), which measures 12½ x 8½ x 11 in., is the most complex of the three sculptures. According to Lynn Urry, this sculpture was "made in the form of an oscilloscope, an electronic measuring device with an old-style round cathode ray tube that I owned at the time. The line emerging from the front of the cylinder is reminiscent of the trace that would appear while the oscilloscope was making a measurement." The clasped sphere impressed Lynn as "being a clasped head in an

'Oh my, what is this?' expression."

Seen from the front, *Untitled* (Gift to Lynn) has a large circular indentation at its upper center, recalling an oscilloscope screen. Two rows of metal cubes, arranged checkerboard style, run across the base of the piece. A found hollow steel cylinder with a rounded end is mounted in the center of the circular indentation with its blunt end facing the viewer.

Protruding between two of the cubes at the bottom of *Untitled* (Gift to Lynn) is a line form that the artist cut with a torch from steel sheet. It ends in two bud-like shapes. This line gives the appearance of passing through the body of the sculpture and emerging at the back, where it meanders sideward and upward, folding back upon itself at one point and then entering the cylinder from behind.

This line seems to emerge from the front of the cylinder, connects to two tiny cubes, and ends in two finger-like shapes welded onto a small metal sphere. A second line with similar forms at its tip seems to clasp the sphere in a different place and then connects to two tiny cubes. The four cubes, the sphere, and the connecting lines comprise a structure that extends out in front of the sculpture.

Even at this very early stage in his career, Steve had begun to employ visual strategies, forms, and images that would become part of his mature work. The circle is a fundamental shape in Steve's art, and there are two in *Untitled* (Gift to Lynn). The first is inset into the front of the piece and the second is the path of the wandering line. These two circles are oriented at 90 degrees to each other, a strategy that claims three-dimensional space.

The metal lines in *Untitled* (Gift to Lynn) are drawings in space that anticipate the cartoonish swoops, wiggles, and intestinal twistings in Steve's later work. Biomorphic forms, which he would employ often, appear for the first time in *Untitled* (Gift to Lynn).

Untitled (Gift to Lynn) is overstuffed and crudely-made. In time, Steve would clarify his ideas and dramatically advance his making skills. *Untitled* (Gift to Lynn) is more important for what it foreshadows than what it contains.

Untitled (Gift to Father) and *Untitled* (Gift to Mother) are also forerunner sculptures. Shaped like a tall pyramid, the 'Father' piece measures 39½ x 6 x 5½ in. One of its three sides is blank except for a decorative vertical line welded onto its surface. The second side has a hollow, box-like form welded onto it 12 inches above the base. This box measures 6 x 4½ x ¾ in. and the artist has cut small designs into its face: two rows of squares arranged checkerboard style, a worm-like line, and bud or leaf forms. The third side also has a welded-on box-shaped form with a bowed-out face and two biomorphic designs cut into its surface. The 'Mother' sculpture is made entirely of wiggly lines of steel that rise from its triangular base to create a pyramidal structure with a bud form at the top.

Tassy and Steve took a watercolor class at the SFAI. She writes that they "traveled around drawing, and brought back the sketches to watercolor." She adds that Steve had "old watercolor paintings in Oakland" and that he "kept a few, but he did not like to do watercolor, did not think he was that good at it."[20] At least two of these works have survived. Both are waterfront scenes, presumably of Sausalito on the San Francisco Bay. *Untitled* (Sausalito) shows a harbor with sailboats and their masts, a pier, and low mountains in the background.[21]

According to Tassy, Steve "worked a lot" on his MG TD convertible because the car was constantly breaking down. He "loved to drive the car through the Berkeley and Oakland hills around lots of curves quite fast with the top down—also across the San Francisco Bay Bridge, with the top down, to our classes."

Tassy quit the SFAI when she gave birth to their son Jay in February 1962. At some

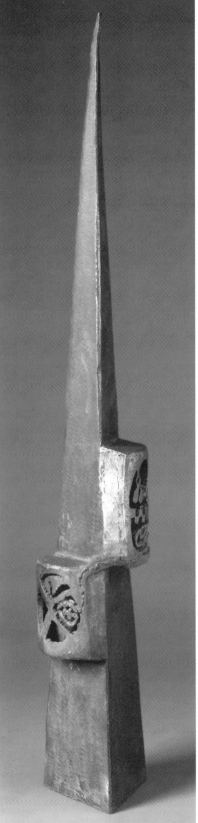

Left and above: *Untitled* (Gift to Father), 1961. Welded steel, 39½ x 6 x 5½ in. Photos by Steve Greiner.

Top and above: *Untitled* (Gift to Lynn), 1961.
Welded steel, 12½ x 8½ x 11 in.
Photos by Steve Greiner.

Alvin Light, *May*, 1962. Hardwoods,
58½ x 72 x 35 in. Photo by Christies, New York.

time after Jay's birth, the couple visited Chicago. She writes that when they returned to San Francisco, Steve "continued his classes in art, and spent more time with new friends and socializing with them at local beer places. My family, after finding out what my situation was, insisted that I come home. . . . [In November of 1962] my dad came and moved me and my nine-month-old son home. Afterward, Steve was not a part of our lives."[22]

Tassy divorced Steve in July 1, 1964. She continued her education, remarried, and became a Bay Area interior designer. Steve took no further interest in his son Jay.

Right Place, Right Time

In June of 1962, Steve exhibited two sculptures in the SFAI Spring Show of more than 200 student works—and there his formal education ended. Until he departed for Chicago in early summer of 1964, Steve kept in close touch with colleagues at the SFAI. According to Janis Urry, friends there let Steve use the studio at any time of day or night to paint or make sculpture. He audited some classes without paying tuition or receiving credit.

San Francisco was an ideal place for a young artist in the early 1960s. Many painters and sculptors who would have major careers—Robert Hudson, Alvin Light, Jay de Feo, Stephen De Staebler, Peter Voulkos, James Melchert, Ron Nagle, Manuel Neri, Harold Paris, William Geis, Carl Gliko, Cornelia Schultz, Rodger Jacobsen, and Carlos Villa—were working and in close touch with each other. There was an exhilarating variety among these artists who seemed to question everything and who stood ready to try anything.[23]

Steve responded to the work of Robert Hudson and Alvin Light, who sought to bring Abstract Expressionism into sculpture. Steve could have seen Hudson's work at the SFAI where Hudson earned a B.F.A. and M.F.A between 1957 and 1963. Hudson exhibited sculpture and drawings at San Francisco's Batman Gallery during 1961. There probably was some casual personal contact between the two, though Hudson has only the vaguest recollections of Steve.[24] Later, in Chicago, Steve told his friend James Zanzi that Hudson had "opened my eyes" and could not say enough good things about his work.[25]

Hudson made funky metal and wooden assemblages, which were often anthropomorphic in form and which incorporated found objects. According to Ron Nagel, Hudson "imposed illusionistic painting on top of metal sculpture."[26] He decorated his work in such bright colors and patterns that one of his sculptures has been compared to "an explosion in a comic book factory."[27] Hudson's anarchic exuberance inspired Steve's early sculptures, many of which look a bit cartoonish, but until the 1980s, Steve had colored only one of his sculptures. Some early Hudson sculptures incorporated lines of cubes arranged checkerboard style, a decorative element that appeared in Steve's work for several years.

According to Jo Farb Hernandez in *The Expressive Sculpture of Alvin Light*, Light was "one of very few significant sculptors to successfully translate the concepts and manners of Abstract Expressionism into three dimensions. . . [he fused the] immediacy and gestural movements of Abstract Expressionism with its more pensive, introspective qualities [to create] an intuitive style that never became arbitrary or formulaic."[28]

Light (1931-1980) received his art training at the SFAI between 1955 and 1961, taught there afterwards, and probably met Steve at the school. According to the artist Rodger Jacobsen, "Light was running the metal sculpture [class] at the SFAI and the work coming out of there was phenomenal . . . it was some of the best sculpture in the country and it remained virtually unknown."[29] Both Steve and Light liked bars, which suggests that they may have met after hours.

Light constructed wooden sculptures from twisty tree limbs and chunks of milled lumber, which he cut, chipped, and scored to activate their surfaces. Some of his unpainted sculptures, which often leaned to one side, were more than nine feet tall. Typically, they were open at their centers, which made them semi-transparent. Light's forms were figural, conical, and occasionally totemic. He could take as long as a year over a single piece, and he was focused on making, rather than selling or building a reputation. Light's scale may have inspired Steve to work large. Like Light, Steve made sculptures with open centers that leaned to one side and he was more interested in making sculpture than anything else.

Another influence was Peter Voulkos who made barbarically powerful clay sculptures and bronze castings. Voulkos joined the faculty of the University of California–Berkeley in 1959 and held court in his "pot palace," which was a basement ceramics studio on campus. Attracted by Voulkos's brilliance and magnetic personality, Stephen De Staebler, Ron Nagle, and Harold Paris worked in the "pot palace."

Steve and Voulkos were on good terms while Steve was living in San Francisco. Lynn Urry recalls a visit with Steve to "an old warehouse down by the railroad tracks" where Voulkos had moved his studio after the "pot palace." As Lynn tells it, "there seemed to be a continual party going on.'[30]

Steve enjoyed the fun, but he also witnessed Voulkos exploring a personal vocabulary of forms, something that Steve would do later in Chicago. Many students assisted Voulkos with his cast bronze sculptures, and Steve may have learned casting fundamentals in that way. Most important, for all his partying, Voulkos was a serious artist, a workaholic, and a superb mentor.

Elaine Smith

Elaine Smith was Steve's companion for much of the time in San Francisco after his formal education ended. They met in Berkeley's Steppenwolf Bar, a folk-singing club where Josh White sometimes performed. Steve was still married to Tassy then, and Elaine accompanied him to divorce hearings. She moved in during September of 1963, and they were together for nine months. According to her, they lived "first in the middle flat of a house on Steiner Street with a weird guy who only ate white rice and listened ENDLESSLY to Billie Holiday . . . and then [in the Primalon Ballroom building at 1223 Fillmore Street]."

Elaine has a photograph of an Abstract Expressionist painting by Steve with a bright yellow sun in it. She recalls a "spectacular welded sculpture called *My Angel Can't Fly* about which I wrote a poem." This sculpture, now apparently lost, was "a big huge thing, with a two-foot diameter circle that was hanging off the frame." Steve was friendly with Light and Voulkos, and he took a ceramics class. He also admired other sculptors such as James Melchert who taught at SFAI, and the painter Jay De Feo.

Steve and Elaine had a Belgium German shepherd dog named Chipper. As Lynn Urry explains, "a Belgium German shepherd, while looking the same, is more than twice as big as a normal German shepherd and is the perfect companion for living in a tough neighborhood." At one point, Steve painted a big canvas that he structured so the eye would move around it in a circle. He was amused to see Chipper viewing his work as intended.

While Steve was living with Elaine, his sister Kay invited them to dinner at her apartment. Steve, who had had an argument with Elaine, arrived alone, entered the apartment, and locked himself in the bathroom. Elaine appeared a few minutes later, called for Steve, and banged on the bathroom door, but he would not respond. "You

Robert Hudson, *T. Table,* 1963.
Enamel and lacquer on steel, 54 x 36 x 36 in.

Robert Hudson, *Log Boot,* 1964.
Enamel on steel, 32 x 21 x 14 in.

couldn't argue with Steve," says Kay. "He was inarticulate and would just run away."

Elaine Smith says that she was "quite committed" to Steve. "He was good at picking people up," she added, "but not good at love. He was a beautiful man, but had no character." He cheated on her.[31]

The Primalon Ballroom

At different times beginning in the 1930s, the cavernous building on Fillmore Street where Steve and Elaine lived housed miniature golf, a dance hall, a German beer garden, a roller-skating rink, and a social center run by the Young Communist League. In 1949, a black couple purchased the structure, named it the Primalon Ballroom, and opened a weekend nightclub where black musicians performed—Count Basie, Lionel Hampton, Billie Holiday, Dizzy Gillespie, and many others. After the nightclub closed, artists moved in and created live-work spaces. The structure was demolished in 1974.[32]

Carl Gliko, a painter who resided in the building for three or four years, remembers it as "quite livable. . . a huge place with skylights and old hardwood floors in poor condition, but this did not matter much to the artists." The rent was $125 per month and everyone shared cooking and bathing facilities. "The artists spent a lot of time talking to each other," Gliko recalls, "and also bickered constantly because they had big egos."

Some "very good artists" lived in the Primalon Ballroom, Gliko adds. Steve "was viewed as a student and did not have high status, but he made little noise and kept to himself." Gliko hardly knew Steve and saw just two pieces in his studio: a big sculpture and a smaller version of the same piece. He does not recall Steve making art very much or taking jobs outside the studio. Some of the artists thought he was a "rich boy from Chicago."[33]

Carlos Villa, who was with Steve at SFAI, remembers him as a "tall skinny guy, shy, with a nice smile." There was "a dialogue going in San Francisco then," Villa says, with Bay Area figurative painters on one side and Hudson, Wiley, William Geis, and Jeremy Anderson on the other.

Steve was "very hard working," Villa remembers, and "was looking at early Bill Wiley and Nathan Olivera in his painting." He mixed his own paints, which was "the San Francisco way." In sculpture, Steve "worked with tough materials," which was "not easy to do." He was "getting what he wanted to get," which was "Abstract Expressionism in three dimensions."[34]

Steve was "in the middle of a lot of things" at the Primalon Ballroom, Villa continues. The building was a "hangout," a "studio enclave," and "all the guys were there." Artists "shot the shit in studios . . . people went to studios to talk . . . the biggest things happened there." Nobody needed bars. San Francisco was not like New York with its artist bars.

Ron Nagel, the ceramic artist, has different memories. Artists talked in bars then and only rarely in studios. "There was no fancy talk," he recalls. "Either you liked it or you didn't—great enthusiasm or disdain."[35]

During the late spring of 1964, Bill Urry visited Steve at the Primalon Ballroom. Soon after, Steve left for Chicago where life would cost less.

[1] The author had multiple contacts by telephone, e-mail, and in person with Steve Urry's siblings. They provided family history, Urry's résumé, press clippings, and photographs. Without their cooperation, it would have been impossible to organize the retrospective exhibition or write this catalog. Rather than stud the text with repetitive footnotes, the author decided to name a sibling when he/she was quoted directly and to footnote other sources.

[2] www.chicago.edu.

[3] Wilbert Lynn Urry (b. 1937) received a B.S. from Purdue University and an M.S. from the University of California in Berkeley. He worked for the University of California Radio Astronomy Department in Berkeley, starting at the very beginnings of research in Radio Astronomy and continued there for more than 40 years. As a senior development engineer, his responsibilities included the design and building of the specialized equipment required for Radio Astronomy for the University's Hat Creek observatory in Northern California. He also collaborated with other observatories such as IRAM, a European Radio Astronomy consortium with observatories in Spain and France, and the Westerborg observatory in the Netherlands. He is the author or coauthor of several academic papers.

Kay Urry [De Marsche] (b. 1942) received a B.A. in art from Mills College, Oakland, California, and later an M.F.A. in drawing from the University of Colorado-Boulder. She taught for many years at Arizona State University in Tempe, where she also served as assistant to the chair of the Department of Art and later as assistant dean of the College of Fine Arts. She also taught at the University of Pittsburgh, the University of Southern Mississippi in Hattiesburg, and at Auburn University in Alabama. Throughout this time she exhibited her artwork nationally and received numerous awards and prizes. For seven years before her retirement in 2009, she was head of the Department of Art at Mississippi State University in Starkville.

Janis Urry [Shefski] (b. 1946) attended the University of Utah, Salt Lake City (1973-76) and graduated from the Rudolph Schaeffer School of Design, San Francisco (1980). Between 1980 and 1985, she did interior design work in Chicago's Merchandise Mart. Since 1985, she has lived in Mesa and Tempe, Arizona, where she was principal of the Designing Eye, an interior design firm. She has also fabricated jewelry, becoming "quite a rock-hound," as she puts it.

[4] E-mail correspondence with Gail Schwartz (Urry) Gestiehr during 2011.

[5] Gestiehr, Ibid.

[6] E-mail correspondence and telephone conversations with Kim Urry Del Giorno during 2011.

[7] Gestiehr e-mail correspondence; Del Giorno, Ibid.

[8] Gestiehr, Ibid. James Zanzi, who knew Steve in Chicago after 1965, confirms that he discovered blues music in high school and adds that he especially liked the Siegel-Schwall blues band. Steve also liked the classics, Zanzi adds, but was less passionate about them. Interview with James Zanzi, April 4, 2011.

[9] Del Giorno, Ibid.

[10] The paintings were offered on September 8, 2002, by Treadway/Toomey Auctioneers, Cincinnati.

[11] Del Giorno, Ibid.

[12] Tassy asked that her last name not appear in this catalog.

[13] 1960-61 Catalogs and Bulletins in the archives of the California College of Arts and Crafts, San Francisco.

[14] Tassy e-mail correspondence.

[15] Jeff Gunderson, library director at the SFAI, photocopied these records for the author. Peter Holbrook, the painter who became Steve's friend in Chicago, cautiously speculates that the bulbous forms in Eastern Art may possibly have influenced forms in Steve's sculptures. As Holbrook told the author in an e-mail, "when Steve was studying Eastern Art (in San Francisco) I was in India examining first-hand the temples and cave frescoes I had studied at Dartmouth. I could show you the paintings from my art school years that employed many of the bulbous forms Steve later put into his sculpture. We were simply on the same page in many ways."

[16] Telephone conversation with Carlos Villa, June 30, 2011.

[17] Lynn Urry remembers a 7 x 7 ft. painting from this time called *The Big Orange Whole*. This "seemed to fit the California landscape," he wrote, "which turns orange in the summer."

[18] Tassy e-mail correspondence. She writes that Steve "laughed when his father said he really liked the gift sculptures."

[19] Tassy e-mail correspondance.

[20] Tassy e-mail correspondance.

[21] The watercolors are owned by Janis Urry. One is in the retrospective exhibition.

[22] Tassy e-mail correspondence.

[23] Ivan Albright, *Art in The San Francisco Bay Area 1945-1980: An Illustrated History*, Berkeley and Los Angeles, University of California Press, 1985. The author drew especially on Chapter 7, "Sculpture of the Sixties."

[24] *Robert Hudson: A Survey*, San Francisco, San Francisco Museum of Modern Art, 1985. Telephone conversation with Robert Hudson, May 2011.

[25] Interview with Zanzi.

[26] Interview with Ron Nagle, July 2, 2011

[27] Ivan Albright, *Art in the San Francisco Bay Area*, p. 149.

[28] Charles Shere, *The Expressive Sculpture of Alvin Light* (Monterey, California, Monterey Peninsula Museum of Art, 1990). The exhibit was curated by Marc d'Estout.

[29] E-mail from Rodger Jacobsen, July 19, 2011.

[30] www.voulkos.com.

[31] E-mail from Elaine Smith Dunlap, September 2, 2010; Interview with Elaine Smith Dunlap, May 30, 2011.

[32] Elizabeth Pepin and Lewis Watts, *Harlem of the West* (San Francisco, Chronicle Books, 2005); Joel Selvin, *San Francisco: The Musical History Tour*, (San Francisco, Chronicle Books, 1996). The Primalon Ballroom must not be confused with the Fillmore Auditorium, which was also on Fillmore Street and the site of historic rock concerts.

[33] Telephone conversation with Carl Gliko, July 15, 2011.

[34] Telephone conversation with Carlos Villa, June 30, 2011. The painter Ron Davis remembers Steve making a "big loopy welded sculpture" around this time.

[35] Telephone conversation with Ron Nagle, July 2, 2011.

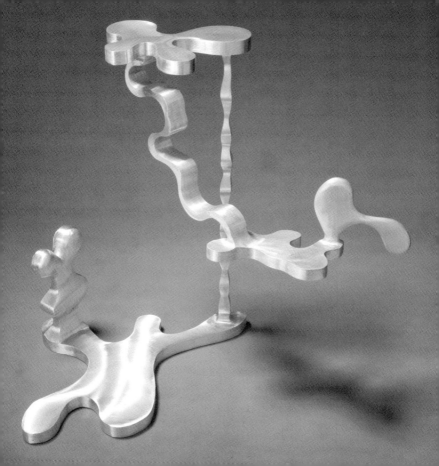

Steve Urry spent nine years in Chicago, from the summer of 1964 until mid-1973 when he departed for New York. It was the most productive time of his life. Working in steel and aluminum, he developed the sculptural forms that had emerged in San Francisco and took them in many directions. His sculpture was so distinctive that people responded at once.

During his Chicago years, Steve had a fabulously successful series of exhibitions. In the summer of 1969, just five years after he arrived completely unknown in the city, the Chicago Museum of Contemporary Art gave him a solo show, its first ever for a local artist. He had six one-man exhibitions in commercial galleries—four in New York and two in Chicago. He was in 18 group shows, mostly in Chicago. He completed commissions in 1968, 1970, and 1971. He won two cash prizes for his work in 1966: $5,000 from the National Council on the Arts and $750 in a local sculpture exhibition. And, in 1967, he won cash prizes of $500 and $200 in the Chicago and Vicinity Show at the Art Institute of Chicago.

Chicago newspapers covered Steve's local exhibitions; *The New York Times* reviewed his shows there, as did *Art in America, Art News, Artforum, Arts,* and *Studio International.* Locally, he was the subject of four feature articles, including a 1971 cover story in *Chicago Magazine.* Two books—*Direct Metal Sculpture* (1966) and *Fantastic Images* (1972)—depicted and described his work.

Sprite

Steve arrived in Chicago with Dolores Marie Thurlby, a pretty hippie who was his common law wife for about five years. Dolores's father was a San Diego tool engineer who also made oil paintings; her mother was half-Choctaw. Dolores was one of their nine children. After growing up in San Diego and attending City College there, Dolores travelled north to the Bay Area to look for work.[1]

Dolores was a nudist.[2] At one point before she met Steve, friends invited her to the Half Moon Bay nudist camp south of San Francisco. While she was there, a photographer took pictures of her outdoors and christened her "Sprite." People at the camp told her of a room for rent on Steiner Street in San Francisco. She was living there early in 1963 when she met Steve, a fellow tenant.

On their first date, Sprite took Steve, fully-clothed, to the Half Moon Bay nudist camp where, as she tells it, "a tall wide Englishman with this big belly and privates flying," ran towards Steve with his hand stuck out in welcome. Steve "wasn't familiar with this kind of thing," she recalls. "He almost freaked out. It was a real eye-opener!"

Steve "was just doing painting" when they first met, Sprite says. She remembers "the beautiful painting with the sun in it" that Elaine Smith photographed. Sprite adds that he made metal sculptures at the San Francisco Art Institute. He took two or three paintings to Chicago, but she thinks that he may have left the sculptures behind.

After a brief stay with a friend, Steve and Sprite moved into the Urry house on 56th Street in Hyde Park. Steve tuck-pointed the house over the summer. It was here, on October 3, 1964, that Sprite gave birth to Jeb Thurlby, her child with Steve. She had a natural childbirth. Steve paid the doctor with a small sculpture.[3]

Professor Urry arranged for the University of Chicago art department to let Steve work evenings in the Lorado Taft Midway Studios on campus. The Studios, which are a 20-minute walk from the Urry house, consist of a large brick barn with two adjoining frame structures. Beginning in 1906, the Studios housed the sculptor Lorado Taft (1860-1936); the University took over the property after his death. Today the Midway Studios are a National Landmark—and an inspiring place to make art! Ivy covers the brick façade. Inside are odd-shaped passageways, numerous staircases, classrooms, galleries, and studios large and small.[4]

Steve probably used shared welders and grinders in the Midway Studios metal

Downstream, ca.1967. Cast and welded,
aluminum, 104 x 90 x 102 in.

shop. According to Sprite, Steve built his first large sculpture there. She recalls an "almost rectangular" base and "a lot of jagged violent-looking edges."The piece was "wide and long... five or six feet high."[5]

Several Midway workrooms have high ceilings to accommodate large sculptures. Artists showed their work in a spacious gallery area near the entrance. Steve exhibited some of his *Round Series* sculptures there in January 1967, and other works in 1968. Midway Studios kept no record of his presence or exhibitions.[6]

Lincoln Avenue Studio

Steve and Sprite stayed with the Urrys for the first few months of Jeb's life and Dion helped with the newborn. Sprite remembers Dion as a "beautiful woman" with "a natural elegance" about her. "I've only met one other woman in my life who had that," she says.

Except for Dion, the Hyde Park Urrys had college degrees, which may have made Sprite feel a bit defensive, but friends said that she had street smarts. Steve once told Peter Holbrook how he and Sprite were "on foot on Chicago's South Side" when a gang of belligerent young blacks confronted them. "They were calling them 'Whitey' until Sprite, with mock dignity, called out: 'I'm not white, I'm PINK!'" That broke up the gang with laughter and the confrontation was de-fused.

"Street smarts wouldn't get you very far at an opening," says Holbrook, "but in the neighborhoods we could afford to inhabit, you couldn't survive without them. Yes, Sprite was feisty alright, but sweet when some trust was established."[7]

At some point in 1965, the couple rented a coach house on Altgeld Street on Chicago's north side.[8] Approximately one year later, they moved a few blocks to the second floor of 2422 North Lincoln Avenue. This is the Biograph Theater building where the bank robber John Dillinger was shot dead by FBI agents after watching a movie on July 22, 1934.[9] Steve worked in the Lincoln Avenue studio, with its tall round-topped windows looking out on the street, for the remainder of his time in Chicago. He is associated with that place in the memories of those who knew him. He was photographed there many times.

Steve and Sprite first shared the Lincoln Avenue space with Bob Silverman, a friend who had helped them secure it. Silverman took the front, covered his walls with burlap, and opened an art gallery. When the gallery failed, Silverman departed, and Steve took over. The couple then had the entire second floor—a space 110 x 60 x 14 ft. —that they divided into a living area and a studio with a wall between.[10] When they moved in, the Biograph Theater featured burlesque shows and Steve took Sprite to see one, her first such experience.[11]

Steve's sole activity in those days was making sculpture. He did not need a job because his parents subsidized him until he had his first major show. According to Sprite, the Urrys felt that they owed Steve something since they had supported his brother Lynn through four years of college. Sprite would rise every morning to feed Jeb. Steve would then get up, say "good morning," take coffee, and disappear into his studio for 12 hours or more. Sprite did all the housekeeping work and says today that she was naïve to demand so little of Steve.[12]

Steve was enormously productive, but it is difficult to make chronological sense of the surviving sculptures. We do not know with certainty whether he built some pieces in San Francisco and brought them to Chicago—or if he made forms in San Francisco and brought them to Chicago for assembly. Since his work at that time was assemblage, the latter seems likely.

Steve worked in an Abstract Expressionist style that grew out of his San Francisco experience and a newer style that emerged in Chicago. Exemplified by *Double X* (1965) and *Blat* (1967), the Abstract Expressionist sculptures were made of steel.

Steve Urry in his Lincoln Avenue studio above
Chicago's Biograph Theater, 1971. In front is an
inflatable, transparent vinyl sculpture.
Photo by Mary Baber.

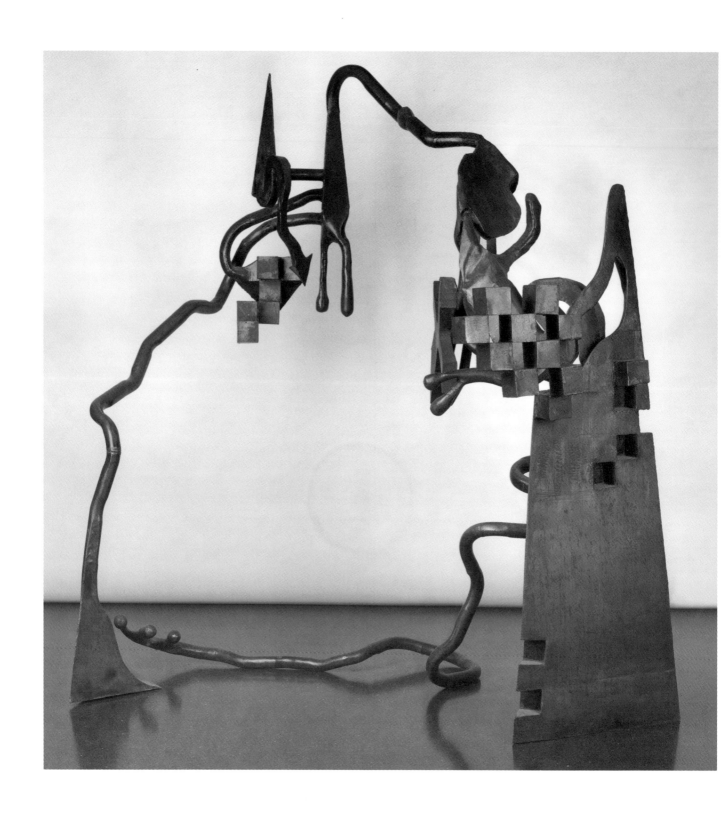

Double X, 1965. Lacquered and welded steel,
83½ x 77 x 42¼ in. Collection of the Museum
of Contemporary Art, Chicago. Gift of Jerry
Peart, 1987.12. Photo by Nathan Keay,
© Museum of Contemporary Art Chicago.

Pieces such as *Head Flower* (1967) were aluminum. The change of material came about because Edwin Bergman, a Chicago art collector and arts patron, allowed local metal sculptors to take all the aluminum they wanted from the scrap yard of U.S. Reduction Co., an aluminum smelter that Mr. Bergman owned in Chicago's south suburbs. Steve, Richard Hunt, John Henry, and others took advantage of Mr. Bergman's generosity. In 1973, Steve presented *Loop and Spiral, NYC* (1971), to Mr. Bergman and his wife. This piece looks like the skeleton of a prehistoric bird.[13]

Double X; Blat

Vaughan Kurtz, a painter friend, visited Steve's studio in 1965 as Steve was making *Double X*. Kurtz remembers that Jeb was then walking, which would put the date in fall. Kurtz and Steve chatted, but did not discuss the work in progress or Steve's intentions for it.[14]

Double X, an 83½ x 77 x 42¼ in. lacquered and welded steel sculpture, is an open circle of welded tube with forms attached. The name apparently refers to the dimensional X form in the sculpture. *Double X* is anchored on the right by a truncated, four-sided pyramid. Emerging from the top of the pyramid are dimensional S and X shapes and tubing that points diagonally upwards. Halfway up, this tube flattens and becomes an oval with tendril-like strips hanging from it. Other strips hang behind the X shape and hold it to the main body of the sculpture.

Past the oval, the tube reaches a peak, bends over, flattens, and turns straight down to end in two hanging fruit-like forms with rounded tips. Three tubes emerge from the left side of the flattened tube. The top tube comes out in front of the sculpture and supports a tall pyramid to which is attached an S-shape turned on its side. One end of this S shape extends downward to make a long rectangular form that ends in a sharply pointed arrowhead.

The middle tube comes down to support a checkerboard form with a slanted back. The bottom tube wanders down toward the floor, where it flattens to make a small triangular base at the far left. Welded to this base are three fruit-like forms and a length of tube that proceeds along an irregular path toward the pyramidal base on the right, which it enters one-third of the way up. Four rows of cubes arranged checkerboard style cross the base of the pyramid.

Ted Garner, a Chicago metal sculptor and master welder who examined *Double X* in company with the author, calls it a "dark, severe, cerebral piece." He thinks that *Double X* was probably made in a corner of Steve's studio, starting with the four-sided pyramid and growing as he assembled it. The pipes are muffler stock cut into short pieces and welded together to make them look bent.

"*Double X* is stick welded," Garner said, "which is an extremely laborious process with much stop and start. Today's artists would use a wire feed welder to do that." Garner imagines that Steve worked by trial and error. He built sub-assemblies, tack-welded them on, viewed the effect, and made final welds once he was satisfied.[15]

Double X looks backward to San Francisco. The checkerboard design at the base of the four-sided pyramid comes from Robert Hudson, and the wandering circular line recalls *Untitled* (Gift to Lynn). Essentially an Ab-Ex drawing in three dimensions, *Double X* works best when read from the front. Steve creates tension in *Double X,* as he does in many other sculptures, by juxtaposing geometric and nature-based forms.

Steve developed the fruit-like forms in *Double X,* using them in later sculptures where they were sometimes compared to the hands of cartoon characters. The open circle, which we saw in Steve's paintings and *Untitled* (Gift to Lynn), appears in different form in *Double X*. The tall pyramid has evolved from *Untitled* (Gift to Father). In *Double X,* Steve's making skills have advanced dramatically over the earlier *Untitled* (Gift to Lynn).

Blat, 1967. Welded steel, 83 x 78 x 42 in.
Installation view, *Art in Chicago:1945-1995,*
Museum of Contemporary Art Chicago.
November 16,1996 – March 23, 1997.
Photo by Nathan Keay, © Museum of
Contemporary Art Chicago.

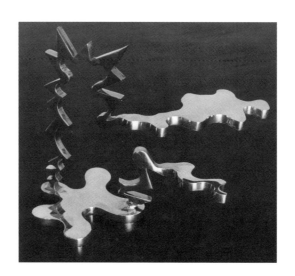

Untraced sculpture in cut and welded
aluminum. Measurements and date
unknown. Visually related to *Blat* (above).

Blat (1967), an 83 x 78 x 42 in. welded steel sculpture that was fabricated after *Double X*, also draws upon Steve's San Francisco history and contains jagged forms that came and went in his work for many years. Essentially a three-dimensional drawing, *Blat* is almost seven feet high with an open center that is wide at the base, pulled in halfway up, and wider again toward the top.

According to a 1971 article about Steve in *Chicago Magazine*, *Blat* was "welded from 16-gauge hot rolled steel using the oxy-acetylene process as well as stick electrode." Steve also used the oxy-acetylene torch "to flame cut hundreds of sections and for hot forming many other parts." The article states that Steve "worked 12 hours a day for two months to produce the piece."[16]

The lines on *Blat's* perimeter suggest lightning bolts, a cartoonish explosion, or possibly the features of some exotic bird. (*Blat* may be the sculpture that Sprite remembered from the Midway Studios.) In 1971, Steve exhibited *Mini Blatt* and *Shimi Blatt*, two sculptures that may be related to *Blat*. Neither work has been traced, but untitled, undated photographs exist of two smallish polished aluminum pieces that might be *Mini Blatt* and *Shimi Blatt*. Each has an open center and a sunburst-like perimeter.[17]

Head Flower

Head Flower (1967), a 108 x 48 x 16 in. cast/welded aluminum sculpture, exemplifies Steve's post-San Francisco style. Flower-like in profile, it sits on a cube-shaped pedestal on top of which is a small cube that supports an upward-curving string of three oval forms that recall fish or frog eggs in a sac. Atop this is a second small cube connected to a tall fishhook-shaped form with a wavy outline. This ends in a yet another small cube connected to a wide, flat ribbon-like shape that folds back upon itself before it proceeds horizontally to end with a still another small cube. Attached to that cube is a second, rather short curved form with a wavy outline that proceeds diagonally upward, but at a 90-degree angle to the ribbon. Two short horizontal extensions come out from the cube that ends the ribbon form, and they terminate in other cubes. Hanging elements on *Head Flower* recall the fruit forms in *Double X*.

As it rises upward, *Head Flower* changes direction four times to occupy vertical space in two dimensions and horizontal space in one. The entire piece looks off-balance and seems ready to tumble down at any moment.

Head Flower is comically anti-monumental. Instead of thrusting up toward the heavens, it bends backward, changes direction, and folds in upon itself as if it cannot make up its mind. Echoes abound in this piece, and the cubes unify it, terminating each part and connecting to the next part. *Head Flower* reads from all four sides. Most of the time, it is photographed from the left or right side and seems gentle. It is more confrontational when viewed from the front.[18]

Head Flower is a much more assured, economical sculpture than *Double X*. Steve concentrates his effects and creates complexity but does not overwhelm the viewer with forms and imagery. The cubes, which were decorative in *Double X*, have distinct formal functions in *Head Flower*.

Five contemporaneous sculptures in similar styles exist in photographs. Two steel pieces—*Check the Pyramid, Xing* (1965), and *1,2,3 Check* (1965) were published in *Direct Metal Sculpture: Creative Techniques and Appreciation* (1966) and were accompanied by text and photographs that illustrate how Steve made them.[19] Both pieces recall *Double X*.

Peter Holbrook and James Zanzi made photos of sculptures in Steve's later style. Holbrook photographed Steve in the Altgeld Street coach house. He stands in front of a two-foot-wide ribbon form that begins on the floor, loops up over Steve's head, bends as it gathers together, bells upward to about 10 feet, and then disappears out of the frame. Behind Steve are cubes and wavy sculptural elements that he apparently fabricated.

Head Flower, 1967. Cast and welded aluminum, 108 x 48 x 16 in. Collection of Elmhurst College, Elmhurst, Illinois. Photo by Rodney Jacob.

1966 Solo Show at Dell Gallery, Chicago.
From left, *Round Six* from *The Round Series*
(1965-66), epoxy-coated steel, 108 x 108 x 30 in.;
Round Five (1965-66) from *The Round Series*,
epoxy-coated steel, 102 x 48 x 6 in.; *Round Two*
(1965-66) from *The Round Series*, epoxy-coated
steel, 48 x 24 x 30 in.
Partially visible at far right is *Oop-Zig.*

Another piece, possibly a finished work, stands in the background blocked from view by
Steve's body.

A second Holbrook photograph, probably dating from 1965, shows Steve in the
Lincoln Avenue studio with its burlap-covered walls. He stands behind *Ribbon Check
No. 1*, a sweeping *tour de force* of a sculpture that is at least 13 feet wide and 12 feet tall.
Suggesting a roller coaster, this piece rises up from its base at the left to a six-foot-high
arch, descends in a mad wiggle to the floor, swoops back up to Steve's shoulder, and
then sweeps out and upward to make a 12-foot-tall loop enclosing a long, slim vertical
void. Steve exhibited this sculpture in Chicago and at the Royal Marks Gallery in New
York during 1967, but it remains untraced. In 1965 or 1966, Zanzi photographed another
untraced piece titled *Red Rubber Ball*.[20]

Biomorphic imagery is so prevalent in Steve's sculpture that we asked Sprite
whether she and Steve ever hiked together in wilderness preserves near San Francisco
or in the forest preserves of Chicago. She recalled walks in Golden Gate Park near
where they lived in San Francisco, but remembered nothing of that sort in Chicago.
The sense of nature and its forms was just "in him," she said.[21]

First Chicago Shows

When he relocated to Chicago, Steve abandoned the thriving Bay Area art scene for
one that could only be termed a work in progress. There were "very few galleries in
the early sixties," says Ellen Lanyon, a painter who helped pioneer opportunities for
Chicago artists in those days. The Art Institute of Chicago took no interest in local art
and the Chicago Museum of Contemporary Art did not open until 1967.

To improve opportunities for themselves, local painters and sculptors founded
Participating Artists of Chicago (PAC), which staged shows that traveled around to
rented spaces. "PAC lasted a couple of years and did a lot," Lanyon recalls.[22]

Steve joined PAC and, in late 1965, exhibited two unidentified pieces in *Phalanx 3,* a show of 85 member artists at the Illinois Institute of Technology. Writing in the *Chicago Daily News Panorama,* art critic Franz Schulze praised Steve's work as "not only superior to nearly all the pieces I had initially seen, but meritorious and provocative in [its] own right." *Joshua Kind,* art critic and historian, wrote in *Art News* that Urry's sculpture gave Phalanx 3 "real distinction."[23]

In May of 1966, Steve's painted metal sculpture *Spring Bubble* (untraced) won the $750 First Prize in *New Horizons in Sculpture,* a show in downtown Chicago.[24] Two months later, Steve exhibited in the PAC-sponsored, all-sculpture *Heavy Show* at suburban Kendall College.

Steve's first solo show in a commercial space opened at the Marjorie Dell Gallery in November. Unlike most Chicago dealers, Dell represented local artists primarily, including Steve and some of the painters who would later be called the Chicago Imagists. Steve showed four epoxy-coated welded steel sculptures, which ranged in height from four to nine feet. They were *Oop-Zig* and *Round Two, Round Five,* and *Round Six* from his *Round Series.*

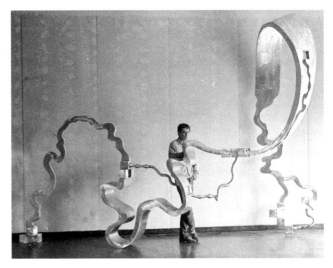

Steve stands in the Lincoln Avenue studio (ca. 1965) behind *Ribbon Check No. 1,* a dramatic aluminum sculpture, at least 13 x 12 ft., that suggests a roller coaster. The sculpture is untraced. Photo by Peter Holbrook.

The untraced *Round Series* sculptures are tall vertical assemblages of cubes, long curving tubes, wavy forms that recall vines, pod shapes with pieces taken out and then set back in, metal forms cut and mounted to suggest that they contain spherical space, and small shapes that connect larger units and serve as accents. One of the sculptures is a corkscrewing arch with its two bases set several feet apart; the other two *Round Series* pieces recall flowers or trees.[25]

Art critic Harold Hayden reviewed the Dell Gallery show for the *Chicago Sun-Times.* "Reshaping his materials so that few traces of their origins remain, [Urry] composes abstractly," he wrote, "playing voids against solids. In the process, he destroys the ancient conception of ideal space defined by a block of stone or wood, as he exploits the ability of steel to penetrate and extend in space."[26]

The *Round Series* sculptures, with their references to living things, look very different from the industrial and architecture-based work of modern masters like Julio González or David Smith. Today, almost 50 years after they were made, Steve's sculptures still look fresh and radical. John Henry, the sculptor who worked as Steve's assistant in 1968, has said that Steve had "the most impressive aesthetic mind I've ever seen." He called Steve a "powerful influence [who] knew no boundaries. There was a sense that anything he could dream up he could build. Ultimately that wasn't true, but none of us knew it at the time."[27]

Late in December of 1966, Steve had another triumph to savor. The National Council on the Arts awarded him $5,000 "in recognition and encouragement" of his work. Steve and Sprite went out dancing to celebrate.[28]

Steve in Altgeld Street studio (ca. 1965) standing among his forms. Photo by Peter Holbrook.

Friends; New York

Two of Steve's close friends in Chicago were the painters Ray Siemanowski (1938-2008) and Peter Holbrook. Siemanowski made colorful semi-abstract paintings of geometric objects floating in room-like spaces. Some shapes in Siemanowski's paintings —cartoonish starbursts, mountains, and circles with wiggly outlines—resemble forms in Steve's sculptures. Siemanowski also made a sculpture incorporating shapes that recall elements in Steve's work. This suggests the possibility of influence, but we have only a few undated images of Siemanowski's paintings and one photograph of his sculpture. With such scant evidence, we can only say that affinities exist between the work of the two artists—and that Steve was much the stronger of the two.[29]

Siemanowski had a solid career, but he drank heavily when young and alcohol

Psychedilly Rose, 1967. Cast and welded aluminum, 126 x 176 x 98 in.

eventually destroyed him. Peter Holbrook recalls a nighttime visit from Steve and Ray in about 1965. "They wanted to go out partying," he writes. "I didn't want to, but loaned them my car . . ."

This car "was a RIGHT HAND DRIVE Austin Healy Sprite (the 'Bug Eyed' model) which Ray had purchased in England and brought back to Chicago," Holbrook continues. "He had started to customize it by molding a beautiful spoiler on the rear deck, but then he lost interest in it and offered to sell it to Steve. Steve couldn't afford it . . . Ray sold it to me instead. Steve and I finished the spoiler and paint job in his coach house garage."

"After extensive boozing . . . a cop pulled the car over for some minor infraction," Holbrook recalls. "Once stopped, Ray (who was driving on the right side) passed out cold. The street was fairly dark and Steve, seeing the cop approach him on the left side, put his hands up on an imaginary steering wheel, showed his license, and told the cop that they just had to go a few blocks to drop off his sleepy friend. Once the cop was gone, Steve carried Ray around to the passenger side and drove back to my place where we revived Ray and had a big laugh."[30]

Holbrook saw a lot of Steve from 1964 to 1970 when he left Chicago for the West Coast. They did odd jobs together like painting houses and hanging commercial signs, and they customized their cars. In those days, Holbrook's paintings looked like nude photographs that he had cut up and collaged onto the canvas. Actually, he took photos from multiple sources, cut and arranged them to his liking, and reproduced this imagery in paint to look collaged. Nowadays Holbrook makes awesome paintings of the Western landscape. He has had a long career and many important shows—and is a perfectly wonderful storyteller.[31]

As Holbrook recalls, "Steve, I think, felt he was in possession of a set of shapes that no sculptor had yet exploited, and that was enough—as many of our teachers would have agreed. Steve used to tell me that I was the 'Last of the Yahoo Painters.' I never asked for a definition, but think that was how he saw himself—the Last of the Yahoo Sculptors. A Free Spirit."

Late in 1966, these two Yahoos decided to take New York by storm. With help from Marjorie Dell, they found a space in midtown Manhattan where they could show their work to prospective clients. Steve purchased a large van and trailer. They packed Holbrook's paintings in a huge crate, which they strapped to the top of the van. They then dismantled Steve's sculptures, piling them in the trailer and the van. The traveling party comprised Steve, Sprite, Holbrook, and his partner Karen. Dion remained in Chicago, taking care of Jeb.

According to Holbrook, the load was "just too much" for the underpowered van, and it broke down almost at once. Back on the road, they had a second breakdown for which repairs took even longer—and cost even more. When they got going again, a blizzard descended on them and followed them all the way to New York. They drove straight through in shifts with two people awake and two asleep on the floors amidst Steve's sculptures.

Once in Manhattan, they installed the work, called on galleries in the mornings, and received visitors in the afternoons. Holbrook remembers "the dealer Alan Stone (whose appraisal of my nudes was that they were too blatant) and William Rubin [later director of the Museum of Modern Art, New York] who lectured us at length on the greatness of his friend Frank Stella." Steve connected with the dealer Royal Marks who scheduled a show for him in October of 1967.[32] Holbrook thought the contract was unfair, but "Steve didn't care—he was on his way. It might frankly be said that we both had our heads in the clouds."

The four met a hippie couple upstairs from their showing space who had "a supply of the most potent weed and some wonderful LSD as well," Holbrook writes. He recalls "a zonked-out evening we spent at a small park nearby where Tony Smith had put up several of his dark monolithic minimal sculptures. They were marvelous by moonlight."[33]

Questing Forest Drawings

Once he returned to Chicago, Steve began working on his show for Royal Marks "from 10 a.m. to midnight, seven days a week, without a single day's break," writes Brian Boyer in a *Chicago Tribune* feature article.[34]

At this time in his career, Steve wanted to present his sculptures in landscape ensembles. There was a hint of this in the Marjorie Dell exhibition with its group of tree-like forms. In 1967 and possibly in 1968, Steve showed his closely related group of *Round Series* sculptures at the Midway Studios. He titled the Royal Marks Gallery exhibition "Ribbon Farm" for the ribbon-like forms in some sculptures and for their presentation as a group of biomorphic shapes. As he was installing "Ribbon Farm," Steve told Boyer that he wanted his work to be a unity. He had similar goals for *Dribblescapes* (1969), his solo exhibition at the Chicago Museum of Contemporary Art, but he did not show another such ensemble until 1976-77, choosing to make pedestal sculptures instead.

Four drawings dating from 1967-68—two named *Questing Forest* and two titled *Questing Scape*—embody Steve's landscape vision and anticipate the sculptures that he would create for *Dribblescapes* and later shows. Of the four drawings, *Study-Questing Forest Elements* and *Questing Forest Study #1* tell us the most.[35]

Study-Questing Forest Elements is a landscape with a river behind. At center, a tall, slim, pointed form with wavy sides pierces a flat cloud. Left of center is a second flat cloud. From each cloud, a wavy tentacle descends toward the ground. At left is a short detached tentacle with a starburst form at its tip. A four-sided shape on the ground recalls a pup tent with openings in its front and side. On the ground at right is a long pyramidal form. The tall slim form at center and the tentacles make this a strongly vertical drawing, while the clouds hover between literalness and suggestions of trees or flowers.

Steve wrote pencil notations on *Study-Questing Forest Elements*. In the upper left is the title: "Study questing forest elements." Beneath it are "#3 foggy range," "#4 clouds," "#5 river," and "#6 flower." At lower left, he writes "Insane pulsing destabilizing of shapes" and "planes and [?? *Text smudged*]." At lower right is "Element #1" and "Ribbon-artist's rendition taken from description of questing beast by harassed victim." These cryptic notations may suggest that Steve was distorting forms from nature.

Questing Forest Study #1 is another landscape with a tent-like form, a tall, slim pyramid, a long cloud, tentacles, a fantasy flower, and shapes on the ground that look like water.

Ribbon Farm

When his work in Chicago was ready, Steve, Sprite ("with thistle flowers in her hair"), and Boyer drove it to New York. Steve wrote "1001 VISUAL THRILLS" on the side of their van. While they were on the road, Steve told Boyer that he "felt like a freak [when he was young] because he thought visually instead of with words. . . "It is hard to verbalize what I am doing," he said. "While I'm working, I have periods when I try to think out in words what I've done. All the things I say about my work, I think out carefully. I think I am trying to show the two things in man—the concrete and the abstract. But these ideas with me are all visual. The visual concept becomes the world, the total thing."

As they were installing the show, Royal Marks complained that eight sculptures were too many, and that visitors wouldn't be able to move around his gallery. Boyer writes that Steve reluctantly pulled out two smaller works, after which "the claustro-

Study-Questing Forest Elements, ca. 1967/68. Graphite on buff wove paper, 275 x 213 mm. Collection of The Art Institute of Chicago. Restricted gift of Mr. and Mrs. Samuel W. Koffler, 1968.459. Photo © The Art Institute of Chicago.

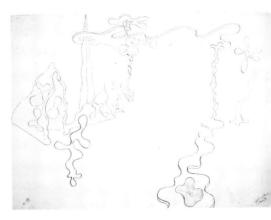

Questing Forest Study #1, Undated. Graphite, with the smudging and erasing, on off-white wove paper, 586 x 827 mm. Collection of The Art Institute of Chicago. Harold Joachim Purchase Fund, 1968.457. Photo © The Art Institute of Chicago.

phobia of the aluminum jungle [lifted], and we [had] an ordered garden."

As they were finishing up, Steve "eagerly [discussed] his art" with Boyer, and revealed "that the same sculptural themes—the cubes, ribbons, and organic forms—recapitulate each other in regular sequence." He explained that, "This is a result of a deliberate creative process that will make the exhibition work environmentally, as a unified spatial area, as well as allowing each piece to work alone."[36]

Ribbon Farm opened October 14, 1967, and was the most important event in Steve's professional life to that point. His father, mother, sister, and son came out on the train for the opening—and some Chicago friends showed up too. Few New Yorkers attended the reception, but when Steve returned to Manhattan a month later, Marks exulted that the show was a "triumphant success" in which everything sold.[37]

Steve showed six pieces from *Ribbon Farm*. We have captioned photographs of five: *Head Flower, Down Stream, Psychedilly Rose, Waul Phaulderawl,* and *Round 6,* a steel piece from the *Round Series*. These sculptures exemplify Steve's late 1960s style.[38]

Steve's undulating ribbon forms invade space without apparent constraint. They sit on the floor, lean on the wall, and soar overhead to startle and delight the viewer. Steve never builds directly upward, but sends his forms in unexpected directions, often turning them 90 degrees along the way. His goal may be to suggest a farm or forest, but it is a place of his own imagining, like nothing we've ever seen before.

Steve got excellent press. Writing in *Artforum,* Max Kozloff called the show "one of the most accomplished debuts it has been my pleasure to witness. The nerve with which these aggregates have been joined together and then crowded environmentally upon each other, is as apparent as the levity of a sculptor who can imagine such titles as *Psychedilly Rose* or *Waul Phaulderawl* . . . his sculptural vocabulary is complex and heroic—even in its detachment. Moreover, an extraordinarily controlled intelligence, wedded with a sharp eye, keeps even the most lavishly abandoned of his ideas within the bounds of sculptural decorum." Kozloff adds that, "one steps over or around or through these compositions, aware of an elasticity of space that is as visceral in tone as it is grandiose in dimension."

The *Art in America* review indicated that Urry "wrings many changes in form in his scribbly, organic-looking structures that sometimes resemble jungle plants gone mad." Grace Glueck in the *New York Times* declared that the show is "not for the tidy-minded." She interviewed Steve who told her that his forms "seem friendly to me. I like to work with shapes that oppose each other. You get extreme opposite things going and if you can put them together it's more exciting. . . a work should have a lasting quality—there should be things in it that you can keep discovering."[39-40]

John Henry

In 1967-68, John Henry worked as Steve's studio assistant, helping to fabricate his sculpture and to create a market for it. Henry, who is known internationally today, began as a painter but switched to sculpture at the University of Kentucky. A graduate fellowship to the School of the Art Institute of Chicago brought him to Chicago in 1966.

Henry saw Steve as a fellow spirit because they both worked big—and they were the only U.S. sculptors to do so in those days. "It was a very intimidating environment," Henry recalls, "because people would say, 'Who'd buy that?' and 'Where are you going to put it?'"[41] To win public acceptance of large-scale outdoor sculpture, Henry deliberately built some pieces for exhibition only, which he later destroyed, reasoning that such sacrifices were necessary to get his work shown. Steve followed Henry's lead, touring his *Headscape* (1968) among local campuses before its destruction in 1970.[42]

Henry teamed up with other artists to organize group shows of large-scale outdoor sculpture and to procure financial and administrative support from the local art establishment. Among the most influential of these shows was, *Eight American Sculptors,* sited in a downtown Chicago plaza during October and November of 1968. Exhibiting artists were Steve, John Henry, Richard Hunt, Jerald Jacquard, Edvins Strautmanis, Mark di Suvero, Michael Steiner, and Michael Hall.

As Henry tells it, a local attorney named Neil Boyer, was "the initial force behind . . . *Eight American Sculptors.* " This exhibition "may have been the first such show anywhere," he adds. "Before this, exhibits usually held work large enough to be shown outdoors, but not specifically built to be shown there." *Eight American Sculptors* was one of several exhibitions and initiatives led by Henry that introduced the public to large-scale outdoor sculpture. It built individual reputations and opened the way to commissions and sales.[43]

Henry has vivid memories of his studio assistantship. "When I was starting out in Chicago," he says, "Steve Urry taught me the spirit of what could happen, that there were no limits. Steve was a master fabricator and aluminum welder, pretty amazing in what he could do. We had a good time working together—in poverty!"

"Steve was a very intuitive artist," he continues, "who never finished college and had little idea of how to find information or use it. Art just came out of him." Hopeless with money, Steve "never made much from his work, spent what he had on booze and drugs, and sometimes left me to pay the rent."

Steve "was one of the dozen best-known sculptors in the U.S. when we worked together, but he could not finish projects. Curators came through the studio to look at his work and offer him opportunities, but this did not seem to matter to him. He did not know how to conduct himself and was his own worst enemy."

The two artists once built a work table, which Steve put at one end of the studio. He piled an overstuffed chair on it and would sit there at the end of the day, smoking weed until he was stupefied, and then go off to bed.

When a big show was coming, the artists worked non-stop. At one point, Steve asked Henry to hire studio assistants, even though there was no money to pay them. "After working 10 to 12 hours running, they fell asleep on the floor," Henry remembers. "Steve came by, kicked them to wake them up, and told them to get back to work. He did not want to deal with people and left this to me, but he could be charming in a bar.[44]

Richard Hunt

Henry introduced Steve to the sculptor Richard Hunt, who was his senior in both age and reputation. Hunt says that the forms in Steve's big sculptures are hollow metal boxes that he welded together. Employing a fabrication technique akin to dressmaking, Steve determined the shape he wanted for his sculpture, made a cardboard form for each piece, laid it on top of a metal sheet, cut out the form with a welding torch, welded pieces together, and then ground and sanded them.

"I work the same way," said Hunt. "It's basic welding and fabrication that we all learn in school. Steve had good making skills, but also had the conceptual ability to go beyond what most people do, to push the limits and come to something new. *Head Flower* was difficult to make because of all the indentations, but that sort of thing is done every day. It's a work of advanced welding and fabrication, coupled with Steve's imagination."

"In the period that we are talking about, everybody worked hard and played hard," Hunt continued. "Steve was willing to work like a dog. To make as much sculpture as he did in the late 1960s and early 1970s, he did lots of welding, grinding, sanding, and polishing."

"Steve was intuitive, not articulate," Hunt continued. "The work was there and you saw his ideas in the work. We talked, but it was mostly shop talk, how to get things done, and never about personal things or art."

Resurrection, 1968. Cast and welded aluminum. Exact measurements unknown, but ground-based portion rises up about 15 ft. and part attached to the building is at least 25 ft. tall. Installed on the façade of the Elizabeth M. Cudahy Library, Loyola University, Chicago (destroyed).

"The key thing is Steve's use of space in the composition of his work," Hunt stated. "He had a spatial imagination and could conceive of how things were composed in three-dimensional space. He was one of several artists who developed a spatial language."[45]

Presentations

During the summer of 1968, Steve, Richard Hunt, and James Zanzi taught an intensive summer workshop at the School of the Art Institute of Chicago (SAIC). Prospective students submitted portfolios of their work, and Steve "got along wonderfully" with one who was a nun. Zanzi, who was on the SAIC sculpture faculty, remembers the class as "terrific." He invited Steve to return in fall for one day each week, but Steve never showed up.[46]

In 1970, Steve was a visiting artist at the Cranbrook Academy of Art in Bloomfield, Hills, Michigan. Michael Hall, who was then Cranbrook's head of sculpture, invited him. Hall, a large-scale outdoor sculptor, visited Chicago often, knew Steve, and exhibited with him in some group shows.

According to Hall, Steve "gave a slide lecture about his work to my students and gave informal critiques [of] their own work . . . It was a good visit. Steve had an easy (shy?) way about him that put students at ease. He had good 'sculpture sense' and was able to say insightful things about much of the work they showed to him."

Hall adds that Steve "was not a teacher. To state that he 'taught' at Cranbrook [or elsewhere] is not correct, and is, in fact, misleading . . . his visits were part of a period effort in which art teachers across America brought 'real artists' into their institutions to let students get a glimpse of the 'real thing,'" Hall continues. "His awkward 'aw shucks,' 'gee, I never really thought about that much' manner conformed perfectly to the stereotype of the artist who makes art because he/she can't 'talk about it, they just do it.' Students like it when their teachers introduce them to artists that they can perceive as the 'authentic' item—the intuitive, non-academic, heroic, anti-social, misunderstood artist/hero of the modernist myth. So the academy served up Steve. But Steve did not teach."[47] He was at Cranbrook for only a few days.

Loyola Commission

Loyola University is a Jesuit Catholic institution in Chicago whose main campus runs north and south by Lake Michigan. In 1968, Steve won a commission to create a sculpture for permanent installation on the façade of Loyola's Elizabeth M. Cudahy Memorial Library.

Steve had submitted a maquette in three parts for a cast and welded aluminum sculpture that he named *Flower Power* and then re-named *Erection.* One part was an undulating ribbon that rose up from the ground to end in a bulbous tongue-like form. A second undulating ribbon started near the top of the maquette and ascended to end in an amoebic form with an open center that Steve positioned directly above the part on the ground. Attached to the wall at left was a large biomorphic form with three finger-like protrusions and a fourth with a hole at its center.

Loyola objected to the name *Erection,* so Steve changed it to *Resurrection.* Loyola was very unhappy when Steve delivered a two-part sculpture instead of what they had ordered. In the piece he built, a ribbon on the ground rose up about 15 feet to end in an amoebic shape with a large hole at its center. A 25-foot-tall companion piece, attached near the top of the library façade, started as a solid circle, then ascended, becoming a gently undulating ribbon that ended in a form like a bird's webbed foot.

Between March 16, 1969, and January 30, 1970, lawyers for Steve and Loyola exchanged numerous letters. Loyola declared that Steve had violated his contract and Steve replied that an artist had a right to change his work, stating that the piece he delivered was better than his maquette. Many years later, Steve explained his

Urry started with aluminum plate (left), bent it to shape, cut the edge into strips, bent and welded the strips together, covered the spaces between the strips with a welder, and ground off the welds to get a smooth surface.

intentions for *Resurrection*: "I was trying to define space—to integrate the grounds with the building."

These words come from *Chicago Sculpture* (1981) by James L. Reidy who talked with Steve in 1979. At that time, Steve said that the Loyola experience had soured him on commissions. "I depend on a process of growth," he stated. "[A]s I'm making the piece, it suggests new things to me, and without that I'm simply a fabricator."

So be it, but Steve had signed a contract and was legally obliged to honor it. In the end, Loyola paid him less than the total contract price. The school also neglected maintenance of the sculpture. About ten years ago, friends visited the site and discovered that *Resurrection* was falling apart. It has since been removed and probably recycled. Steve completed other commissions without incident.[48]

Dribblescapes

On July 19, 1969, Steve's *Dribblescapes,* an exhibition of five new cast and welded, aluminum sculptures, opened at Chicago's Museum of Contemporary Art. According to a Museum press release, *Cloud Flower* and *Cloud,* which strongly resemble forms in his *Questing Forest* drawings, were entirely suspended from the ceiling. *Ribbon-Flowering Dotscape* (whose name Steve changed to *Moon Ribbon* in honor of the Apollo landing) and *Polka-Dotted Earth Mother* operated between the floor and ceiling, spreading out into individual disks and dome-shaped elements that Steve called "polka-dot fields."

Dribble Dot, the smallest piece, grew out of a polka dot field. The Museum quoted Steve: "The whole series has to do with hemispheres. I am working with the polka dot as a repetitive pattern contrasted with seemingly free-form shapes that relate to them."

Continuing, Steve said: "I do a lot of drawings, pick out shapes, make the shapes, and do more drawings. It's like a growing process. I spend a good deal of time trying to pick out different space relations, to fit shapes together differently. Nothing ever quite comes out the way it was first planned."[49]

Steve imagined the forms of his two cloud sculptures in his *Questing Forest* drawings of 1967-68 and built them for *Dribblescapes*. Steve made many drawings throughout his career. He made some to design his large sculptures, developed ideas in sketchbooks, and exhibited drawings next to his sculptures in gallery and museum shows.

Dribblescapes was installed in the central areas of the Museum's upper gallery and commanded its space. *Moon Ribbon* and *Polka-Dotted Earth Mother,* two of the most beautiful sculptures that Steve ever made, gave *Dribblescapes* an otherworldly quality.

The brightly polished, 30-foot-wide *Moon Ribbon* is a long slim piece whose center rests on the floor. On the right side, an undulating ribbon gently rises to about five feet above the floor and ends in a rounded tip. On the left is a form resembling a huge ladle with liquid pouring from it. A long bent pole connects ladle and base.

Polka-Dotted Earth Mother is a 16-foot-wide floor piece that starts on the left with two dome shapes surrounded by a base. This leads to an undulating ribbon-like form that supports a large triangular flag-like shape of slim profile with two dome-shaped

Dribblescapes solo show at the Chicago Museum of Contemporary Art, 1969. All works were made in 1968 or 1969.

Large Cloud, cast and welded and hammered aluminum, 35 x 15 ft., is attached to the ceiling. The large piece on the floor at left is *Polka-Dotted Earth Mother,* cast/welded and hammered aluminum, 16 x 4.6 x 8 ft. In the center of the floor is the multi-piece *Dribble Dot,* cast/welded and hammered aluminum which covers a 48 in. square area. The large ladle-like sculpture at the back is *Moon Ribbon,* originally titled *Ribbon Flowering Dotscape,* cast and welded and hammered aluminum, 308 x 96 x 120 in.

Attached to the ceiling is *Cloud Flower,* also known as *Small Cloud,* cast/welded and hammered aluminum, 15 x 10 x 5 ft.

voids in it. Studio photographs of a large ladle form (presumably *Moon Ribbon* in progress) suggest how Steve made this double-walled fantasy shape. He started with plate, bent it to shape, cut in strips at the edge, bent and welded these strips together, filled in the leading edge with a welder to cover the spaces between strips, and then ground the welds off to get a smooth surface.[50] Sculptors wince at these photographs for they know how laborious Steve's process was. The polka dot forms in the MCA show were disks of aluminum sheet that were spun over a mandrel. Steve may have purchased seconds from a specialist fabricator, or he may have had them made to order.[51]

Writing in the *Chicago Daily News,* the art critic Franz Schulze called *Dribblescapes* a big, bumptious, blowzy, and emphatically undecorous mélange . . . . Like many Chicago artists of his generation . . . Urry is charmed by pop-shape: by the two-dimensional amoeboid forms that one associates with the balloons, the sweat drops, the fingers and the toes, the benday patterns, and the like, of cheap comic strips."

"These forms he has now molded into a veritable walk-through environment of loops and scoops and drips and slurps and 'ribbons' and 'polkadots,' a welded-and-cast aluminum garden of whimsical volumes and spaces at times erotic, at times crass, but always informed with a strong, ironically comic authority."

"If [Urry] shares all these stylistic attributes with his Chicago colleagues," Schulze continued, "he is distinctly different from them in the aggressive and monumental scale to which he has raised this rather simple vulgar vocabulary.'[52]

Schulze was to republish this account of Steve's work almost verbatim in *Fantastic Images: Chicago Art Since 1945* (1972), a heavily illustrated critical history that featured accounts of 18 Chicago artists and their work. Steve's part of the book is illustrated with full-page-sized photographs of nine of his sculptures. In his introduction to *Fantastic Images,* Schulze sees Steve as an artist who seems to have learned "as much from the brittleness of cartoon art as from modern museum painting.'[53]

Schulze visited Steve "once or twice" in the Lincoln Avenue studio, which was much larger than those of other artists, some of whom were painting in their apartments. Schulze found Steve "very likeable" and thought him "very nice looking." Steve agreed with what Schulze had written about him and acknowledged that Chicago art and comic strips had influenced his work. Schulze concluded that Steve was "a guy who made things, who followed his own star. The fact that he made a sculpture was what mattered to him."[54]

Zabriskie Gallery Show

On October 21, barely six weeks after *Dribblescapes* came down, Steve opened a show at the Virginia Zabriskie Gallery in New York. It included *Moon Ribbon, Polka-Dotted Earth Mother, Large Cloud, Small Cloud,* and an untitled sculpture. Eight days later, he formally consigned five additional cast welded aluminum sculptures to the gallery, along with 11 pencil drawings.

The pieces from *Dribblescapes* were all quite large, ranging from the untitled piece (10 x 8 x 8 ft.) up to the suspended *Large Cloud* (35 x 15 ft.). The second batch of works—all pedestal pieces and presumably easier to sell—ranged from *Vacuole* (14½ x 13½ in.) up to *Large Winged Thing* (75 x 51 in.). (The third measurements for the last three pieces were not given.)

The Virginia Zabriskie Gallery was a big step up after Royal Marks. Zabriskie opened her gallery in 1954, and over the next 15 years developed it unto a venue for top New York artists, including many sculptors. She apparently did well with Steve, whom she showed again in 1972, 1973, and 1976. It is likely that she kept a stock of his work on hand. Steve also consigned work to her that was not listed as part of his shows. Zabriskie published catalogs for many of her artists but only one promotional was produced piece for Steve.[55]

The critic for *Time Magazine* wrote of the Zabriskie show that Steve has "the kind of outlandish ideas that a safer and saner sort would instantly abandon." The writer for *Art News* noticed "the brightness of [his sculptures'] surfaces; the texture of finish . . . the gravity-defying lunges into space; [and] the platforms making puddles of metal below the ceiling or along and above the floor. . . Each work is a kind of journey along a flaccid edge until one notes that the surrounding space activated by the work is not flabby."[56]

Experiments and explorations

After 1969, Steve abandoned large-scale sculpture for seven years.[57] The San Francisco influence seemed to disappear as he explored his visual vocabulary in smaller works, experimenting with scale, materials, ways of building up, surface, and fabrication. As he concentrated his forms, his work gained strength and his effects became more subtle. Chicago art critics saw his shows and wrote about them.

Steve worked with many different forms, the most important of which were the cloud and the arch. Related to the cloud is the "splat," which is the name we give to the shape that results when a semi-liquid object like a tomato or raw egg is dropped on the ground.[58]

Other forms include the "winged things" that have bases like webbed feet and tall, flat bodies that recall penguins.[59] A tulip-like form (Steve called it "puckering") with leading edges that suggest lips, evolved from the scoop in *Moon Ribbon* (1969). Some of Steve's sculptures have low square bases and curving ribbons of metal that spiral up from the center. He also created a few unique pieces that apparently embody ideas he tried out, but did not pursue.

The Cloud Forms

Clouds and splats appeared in Steve's work two years before *Dribblescapes*. A long, tongue-like shape with a wavy outline serves as the base for *Hi* (1967), a cast welded aluminum piece that looks backward to San Francisco. *Hi* has a small cube at its center, a large cube at one end with bud-shaped voids in it, and a meandering length of tube that joins the cube at center to its smaller end. After *Hi*, cubes disappear from Steve's sculptures.

Small cloud forms appear in *Fear and Expectation* (1968), a 31-inch-high cast and welded aluminum piece in which Steve elevates two clouds on posts resembling inverted funnels. The elevated clouds suggest platforms or shelves. Steve experimented with cloud forms, making them thick or thin, giving them flat or triangular undersides, and sometimes just creating an outline in aluminum strip.

In 1969, Steve made a cartoonish, wildly fanciful aluminum sculpture with three cloud forms, which he presumably sawed from plate. This untitled work is in the collection of the Chicago artist, Claire Prussian (see page 16). The base of this sculpture is a cloud; two other cloud forms are elevated. A wavy post holds up the highest form and a metal ribbon projects out at an angle beneath it to support a second, smaller cloud situated about halfway up the sculpture. A slightly tilted shape, like Steve's familiar bud forms is welded onto the base. On a corner of the smaller cloud is a flat spigot-like form with a rounded outline that recalls the "winged things."

This piece invades space in many directions as it thumbs its nose at the world. All the gravity-defying, space-contorting effects that Steve created with his larger sculptures are present in this work, but reduced in scale and intensified.

Prussian remembers seeing this piece "somewhere" and calling Steve up; he brought over the sculpture right away. She found Steve attractive and amiable. The sculpture has been a prized possession ever since.[60]

Angling Cloud Plane (1970; untraced) is pure fantasy with a long, narrow wavy base

Popeil Commission, 1968.

Loop and Spiral, NYC, 1971.
Cast and welded aluminum, 40 x 70 x 42 in.
Collection of Robert Bergman.
Photo by Steve Greiner.

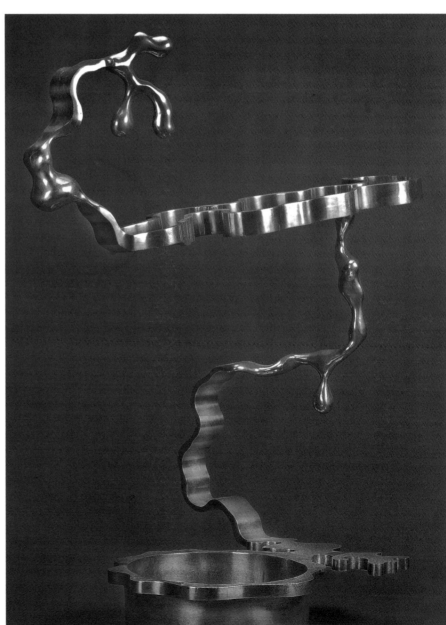

Untitled, 1970.
Cast and welded aluminum, 34 x 40¾ x 22¼ in.
Collection of the Smithsonian American Art
Museum. Gift of the S.W. and B. M. Koffler
Foundation,1979.53.32.

and a post at one end that recalls a golf club supporting a highly polished flat cloud shape tilted at a 45-degree angle. Above the cloud is a long intestinal post with a strange glob of metal at its tip. Steve put a phallic shape at the other end of the base.

The Smithsonian American Art Museum owns an untitled 34 x 40¾ x 22¼ in. cast and welded aluminum sculpture from 1970 (see page 34) that has a shallow cylindrical base with a small cloud form welded to its side. Emerging from one end of this cloud is a metal ribbon bending backward upon itself as it rises. Attached to the end of the ribbon is a reversed L-shaped cast support with a metal teardrop hanging from one side.

Above is a cloud outlined in formed aluminum strip. Steve attached an upward-pointing ribbon combined with a cast piece, topping off his sculpture with a biomorphic form that recalls arthritic fingers or some kind of plant part. This *tour de force* sculpture ascends in its own way, following no known rules.

In two larger cloud sculptures, Steve used polished aluminum plate and slim profile support posts to make works that seem to fly. *Affirmation* (1971), 53 x 28 x 38 in. has a "splat"-shaped base with a wavy main support post topped by a large cloud form with an open center, formed and cast posts supporting a second, much smaller cloud form, and a large hand-like shape on a wavy post.

In addition to the above, Steve made sculptures with loose, irregular bases that resemble eggs in a frying pan. There is much humor in this work.

Untitled (Open Arch Over Column Topped By Cloud Form), signed "Urry 71" with circled number 7 (etched into base). Cut, welded, formed aluminum, 16½ x 13 x 14½ in. Collection of Barbara and Erwin Glass. Photo by Greg Heck.

The Arch Forms

One of Steve's early arch-form pieces was the *Popeil Commission* (1968). He made this 64-inch-high polished aluminum sculpture (see page 33) for Samuel J. Popeil (1915-1984), the co-founder with his brother Raymond (1921-1988) of Popeil Brothers, Inc., which manufactured household gadgets including the Veg-O-Matic, Kitchen Magician, and Miracle Broom. Popeil products were sold in huge quantities through fast-paced demonstrations on television. "It chops, it slices, it dices" became the byword for the popular Veg-O-Matic, which was eventually forced off the market when the humorless U.S. Federal Trade Commission determined that it could not do the things it claimed. For a while, the Popeils were rich, but their firm and a successor eventually went bankrupt.[61]

The *Popeil Commission* appeared in *Fantastic Images* and in photographs of Steve's studio, but it has proven impossible to trace. Pamela Popeil, Samuel's daughter, was a teenager at the time of the commission and showed us photos of the family apartment. The sculpture is not present in the photo, and no surviving Popeil family member recalls seeing it, which suggests that the commission was completed but that the Popeils did not take delivery. To add to the confusion, the *Popeil Commission* does appear in photographs of the Lincoln Avenue studio in the early 1970s. Steve showed the piece in the *Chicago Imagist Art* exhibition in May and June of 1972, where it is listed in the catalogue as made in 1971 and "Lent by Mr. and Mrs. Samuel Popeil, Chicago."

Untitled (Spiraling Up), signed "Urry 71" with circled numeral 9 (etched into base). Cut, welded, formed aluminum, 8½ x 12 x 8³/₄ in. Collection of Barbara and Erwin Glass. Photo by Greg Heck.

Pamela Popeil remembers an aluminum chess set (see page 36) that Steve made in 1968 on commission. The Popeils kept the set in the den of their apartment where it took up a lot of room. "I hated it," Pamela recalls, "and constantly complained about it."

Whatever its fate, the *Popeil Commission* is one of Steve's intestinal sculptures, with a lumpy, tubular body that's wavy in outline. The intestine shape recalls the form in *Head Flower* that we likened to fish eggs in a sac. Steve used intestine forms often in the late 1960s and early 1970s. He apparently made them from lengths of aluminum tube that he welded together. Next, he added filler to complete the form, sanded the piece down, and gave it a high polish.

Following the *Popeil Commission*, Steve made arches in a variety of materials and scales. *Michelle's* (1969) is a 28-inch-high leaning arch that stands on a cloud-form

From the *Popeil Chess Set*, 1970. Cast and formed aluminum, (seven pieces, 2½ to 7½ in. high). Collection of Pamela Popeil, Chicago. Photo by Steve Greiner.

Untitled Waxes (Arch),1970s. Black wax, 11 x 4¾ x 3 in.; *Leaning Arch*, 1970s. Black wax, 14 x 10½ x 2½ in. Collection of Sedgwick Studio. Photo by Steve Greiner.

base. The left side is intestinal, but with wider, flatter lumps than the *Popeil Commission*, and the right side is tubular. An undated, untitled bronze piece is arch-shaped and about 2½ feet tall, with a "splat"-like outline. This sculpture, which is wider and flatter than the *Popeil Commission,* has a consistent gauge, which suggests that it was formed from heavy plate. In 1972, Steve cast a 15-inch-high arch piece in bronze.

In 1971, Steve exhibited his 10-inch-high *Art Deco Piece* at the Zabriskie Gallery. Its welded aluminum shape, with its pulled-in bottom, wide center, and round top, suggests a human face. Steve made *Art Deco Piece* from four nested arch shapes that he welded to a "splat"-like base. A somewhat similar piece appears in photographs taken in Steve's studio in the early 1970s.

In 1973, Steve made his grandest arch sculpture, *Arch,* a 21-foot aluminum work painted white. It was purchased by the City of Muskegon, Michigan, where it is prominently displayed (see page 41).

Steve also made some half-arch forms, about 18 inches tall. They rise straight up from their bases and have "splat" outlines with tops that recall fingers spread apart. Steve cut one of these pieces from aluminum plate; the other, which he dated 1972, was cast in translucent pale green Plexiglas. In 1972, he also cast some pyramidal pieces in Lucite, one of which he gave to his brother.

Other Forms

Steve showed *Vertical Spiral* (9 x 9 x 10 in.) at the Zabriskie Gallery in 1971. According-ing to the metal sculptors who knew him, Steve cut these pieces out with a saw, fastened them to a work table, pulled up the free end to make the spiral, and gave the work a high polish. It is likely that he made several such spiral pieces, but we only have photographs of two.

Among Steve's other oddities is the highly polished 36-inch *Flagging Tower* (1969), which is set on a small dome-like base. The "flagpole" is a twisty construction of polished aluminum and the "flag" points diagonally upward.[62] Photographs exist of an unidentified, untraced heavy dome-like casting with four rounded, cloverleaf-like openings in its top. Other fanciful sculptures include an untitled bridge-like form (1970), an untitled cast piece (1970) that could be cartoon fingers or a plant, and five cast teardrops (1970). The teardrops don't resemble anything else that Steve ever made. Maybe he did them for fun.

Phyllis Kind

On November 12, 1971, Steve opened a show of smaller sculptures at the Phyllis Kind Gallery. Kind had opened her gallery in 1967, initially dealing in master prints. When Marjorie Dell closed her Chicago gallery and moved to New York, Kind began to represent younger artists including Steve and the Chicago Imagists. Steve consigned six sculptures to Kind in June of 1971.

Kind prepared a poster for the show, which depicted Steve in his studio dwarfed by his sculptural forms. She advertised his work in *Artforum* and *Art News*. Michael Hall remembers this "very lively" exhibition and that "the place was packed" for the opening. "The show was all small aluminum works and I think some sold," he adds. "Steve was in good spirits and happy to have his friends and admirers around."[63]

Jane Allen and Derek Guthrie reviewed the Phyllis Kind exhibition for the *Chicago Tribune,* stating that the work shows him trying to "integrate his earlier style with the mainstreams of 20th century art. In some ways the exhibition can be interpreted as Urry's flirtation with major trends in abstract sculpture, stopping short after David Smith."

Allen and Guthrie add that Steve's sculpture "treads a line of balance between con-struction and fluid organic flow. The large pieces tend to break down under the stress of construction because the contrast between the thin supporting rods and the free shapes resembling Walt Disney puddles is too great. There are too many changes in rhythm. . . . in spite of this, Urry's control of space and sensuousness of surface pulls them together."

The smaller works "are more experimental and show a wider range of ideas and styles. They are like three-dimensional sketches except that their surfaces are as finished as the larger works." Later they praise "Urry's direction in developing his own formal vocabulary without conforming to dominant trends and his sensitive use of material."[64]

Zabriskie and Others

Soon after the Phyllis Kind show came down, Steve opened his second exhibition at the Virginia Zabriskie Gallery (February 8, 1972). He showed the *Art Deco Piece, Vertical Spiral,* and (judging by their titles) some of the "puckering" sculptures.[65]

The reviewer for *Arts Magazine* wrote that Steve's "ribbons seem to be alive, crawling along the floor or sprouting at higher levels. These moving ribbons sometimes have snake heads or, at other times, resemble vines. . . . they usually expand and grow from a central point helping us to define the space of the room." David Shirey, in his *The New York Times* review, took note of Steve's reduced scale and wrote that his "constructions are like solid ribbons or cloud formations arranged in various ways through space. They have an improvisational character . . . that makes them resemble sketching or scribbling in air."[66]

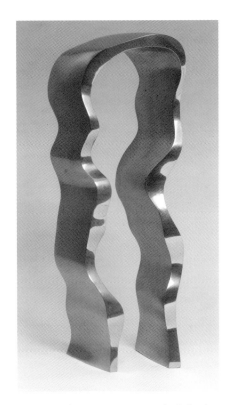

Arch, 1972. Cast bronze, 15 x 5 x 5 in. Collection of the David and Alfred Smart Museum of Art, The University of Chicago. The Joseph P. Shure Collection. Photograph ©2012 courtesy of the David and Alfred Smart Museum of Art, The University of Chicago.

While he was exhibiting solo in commercial art galleries, Steve had work selected for important Chicago group shows that helped strengthen his local reputation. In 1967, 1971, and 1973, he participated in the *Annual Exhibition of Artists of Chicago and Vicinity,* a competitive catalogued show at the Art Institute of Chicago. For many years, and particularly when Steve was just starting out, the "C&V" was an important stepping-stone in local art careers because the Chicago gallery scene was so small. As exhibition opportunities improved, the "C&V" diminished in importance and the Art Institute ended it in 1985.

In May and June of 1972, Steve showed *Check the Pyramids Xing* (1965), *Downstream* (1966), and the *Popeil Commission* (1969) in *Chicago Imagist Art,* a catalogued exhibition at the Chicago Museum of Contemporary Art. In his catalog introduction, Franz Schulze writes that Steve "works abstractly most of the time [and] shares a proclivity toward intestinal forms and cartoon-balloon shapes that identifies him with the funkier aspects of recent Chicago art." Schulze does not apply the term Imagist to Steve or his works. The Imagist artists were painters.[67]

In September of 1972, Steve exhibited *Downstream* (1966) and an unidentified large-scale sculpture from 1965 or 1966 in the plaza of One Illinois Center, a high-rise complex in downtown Chicago. This exhibition was reviewed in the *Chicago Daily News Panorama* by the art critic Dennis Adrian in a feature article entitled, "Let's Show Off More Sculpture Downtown Like Steve Urry's. 'Though this was a minor show, Adrian wrote so perceptively—he was the best art critic to write about Steve's work— that we quote him at length.[68]

Untitled, 1971. Cast aluminum, 9¼ x 10 ½ in. Collection of the David and Alfred Smart Museum of Art, The University of Chicago. Gift of Mrs. Marion Simon. Photograph ©2012 courtesy of the David and Alfred Smart Museum of Art, The University of Chicago.

"[T]here is no doubt that [Urry] is in full possession of very considerable powers of esthetic invention and technical ability," Adrian began. "Each of the two 10- or 12-foot pieces uncoils wriggling organic shapes of welded and cast aluminum, punctuated here and there with conceptual geometric solids that halt and give resistance to the looser shapes that are associated with natural forms."

"The virtuosity of Urry's sculptural ability comprises several difficult areas," Adrian continued. "He draws the eye (and sometimes the rest of the viewer) through and around the muscular sinuosities of his characteristic forms, and articulates complex rhythms of volumes and voids to provide an exceptionally exciting awareness of an elastic space inhabited by shining dynamic volumes."

Clockwise from top left:

Untitled (Biomorphic forms). Signed "S. Urry 70." 6¾ x 1¾ x 11 in. Collection of Janis Urry. Photo by Steve Greiner.

Untitled (Three fingers). Signed "S. Urry 70". Cast aluminum, 7¾ x 8½ x 1¼ in. Collection of Janis Urry. Photo by Steve Greiner.

Untraced "puckering" sculpture in cut, formed, and welded aluminum.

Winged Thing. Signed "S. Urry 69".(Purchased, October 16, 1969). Cut and welded aluminum, 30 x 15 x 9 in. Collection of Playboy Enterprises, Los Angeles. Photo by Steve Greiner.

Untitled (Ivory-colored sculpture), 1969. Signed "For Kay 1969." Cast and welded aluminum, ivory paint, 16½ x 12½ x 6¾ in. Collection of Kay Urry DeMarsche. Photo by Steve Greiner.

Untraced "spiraling up" sculpture in cut, formed, welded aluminum.

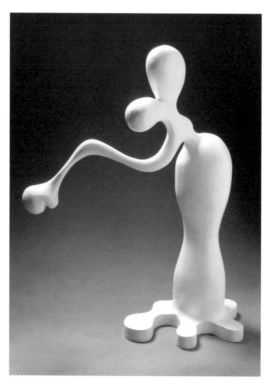

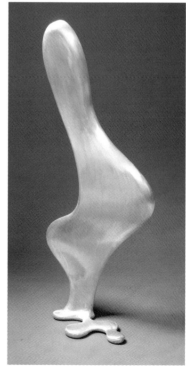

"There is an intensely physical, almost balletic quality to Urry's involvement with space and its displacement, and his lolloping, bounding forms project a wonderfully harmonious recollection of the forces of organic growth in nature, specifically as landscape."

Adrian then calls Urry's subject "a kind of cosmic landscape experience" and adds that only Mark di Suvero, Anthony Caro, and Richard Hunt "can put forth languages of form which make space dynamic as fluently, clearly, and powerfully as does Urry."

Michelle

Sprite recalls that she and Steve met Michelle in November of 1966 at the opening of Steve's Marjorie Dell Gallery show. Michelle was then married to Jack Altman. The Altmans later invited Steve and Sprite to dinner at which the Altmans had a fight. Steve and Michelle were drawn to each other and Sprite, sensing that her time with Steve was ending, apparently moved out of the Lincoln Avenue studio in 1968, taking Jeb with her.[69]

Sprite found work as a Nurse Aide at Chicago's American Hospital and saved enough money to return to California with her son. The Altmans divorced on August 11, 1969; Michelle and Steve married in 1970.

After their marriage, Steve and Michelle bought a house in Chicago's suburbs so that Jeb, after spending the school year in California with his mother, could summer with his father. Once Steve and Michelle moved to New York in 1973, "he just stopped communicating with us," says Sprite. "I think that had more to do with Michelle than with Steve. Jeb did not live with them in New York. There was no communication." In San Diego, Sprite "got into hair," worked as a hairdresser, married, and had a second child. She now lives in Hawaii.

Michelle Dorothy Kaplan [Altman] (1939-2006) was born in Winnipeg, Manitoba, the daughter of a clothing manufacturer. As a child, she loved comic books and had a big collection. Michelle graduated with a degree in English from the University of California Los Angeles, opened a dress shop in Los Angeles, made a success of it, sold it, and moved to New York intending to conquer Seventh Avenue. When that effort failed, she relocated to Chicago where she found administrative work at *Playboy* magazine. At one point, she lived in the Playboy mansion and mothered bunnies-to-be. Hugh Hefner, *Playboy's* founder, was her boss but never her lover.[70]

Michelle met Steve while she was *Playboy's* associate cartoon editor. In 1972, Hefner promoted her to chief cartoon editor, a position she held until her death in 2006. Each week, she reviewed 1,000 cartoon submissions. Her choices—not all were smutty—helped *Playboy* build a reputation for its excellent cartoons.

Michelle was a driven person who triumphed on her own terms in an environment where women were viewed as sexual playthings. Well paid, Jewish, and a feminist with social ambitions, she was an improbable match for Steve. By 1969, she was typing his letters. They married in 1970 and honeymooned in Mexico.

Michelle and Steve decorated the Lincoln Avenue studio with cloth and vinyl hangings and a large, cloud-shaped aluminum coffee table that was likely a *Dribblescapes* sculpture because it stands on tin cans instead of legs. The photographer Peter Bradshaw remembers photographing the pair in 1971 "under Michelle's art direction."[71]

Janis Urry was living out of town when Michelle replaced Sprite, did not like Michelle when they met and never accepted her. But Steve said that Michelle was the only woman he had ever married willingly. He chose her for his wife, loved her, and was faithful, but she had the money and the control.[72]

In a 1973 feature article about her in *New Woman* magazine, Michelle, who was then separated from Steve, said that she needed a "profound" love relationship in her life, but wanted to work too. "I think work is a catharsis, a challenge, and it brings development and growth," she stated.

Untitled (Gift to Lynn). Signed "S. Urry 72 for Lynn". Cast Lucite, 8 x 4¾ x 3 in. Collection of Lynn Urry. Photo by Steve Greiner.

Untitled (Gift to parents). Signed "S. Urry 72" (inscribed to parents). Pale green cast Lucite, 18 x 6½ x 1¾ in. Collection of Janis Urry. Photo by Steve Greiner.

Untitled, early 1970s. Manipulated Polaroid photograph of industrial scene, 10 x 10 in. Collection of Janis Urry. Photo by Steve Greiner.

"For a while," the *New Woman* article continues, "living and sharing worked out well. But living together is not marriage when he's thinking one way and she another. And as Michelle became more and more involved with her career, they found themselves unwilling to cope." An "amicable" separation resulted. Michelle said that she loved Steve, but wanted to live in "separate stables," adding that she wanted to have a baby.

This was the situation in January of 1973, when the sculptor Jerry Peart became Steve's studio assistant. Steve's lease was up in August and he was considering a move to New York where he felt national recognition awaited. Michelle promised to finance a studio in Manhattan if Steve contributed his sweat equity. She also wanted a baby and Steve figured that he could handle that.[73]

Sculpture Off the Pedestal

Early in 1973, Steve and Jerry Peart built *Arch,* a 21-foot-high aluminum sculpture painted white that he designated for *Sculpture Off the Pedestal,* a catalogued group show of large-scale outdoor sculptures that occupied downtown Grand Rapids, Michigan, from September 8 to December 3, 1973. This show originated in a lecture that Michael Hall gave at the Grand Rapids Art Museum (GRAM) in 1971.

As Hall tells it, he talked about "forms of sculpture that could meet a viewer in a shared space [which] was a pretty new idea at that time." In selecting visuals for this lecture, he "found some illustrations of sculpture on a pedestal and described it then as . . . having its own discrete space and the pedestal functioning for the sculpture much as a frame functions around a picture to . . . buffer the encounter between the object and the environment." Next, he suggested that one could remove this buffer and "let the [sculpture] confront the environment directly."[74]

"Most of the [recent] thinking in American sculpture" has gone in that direction, Hall continued. He had in mind the shows of outdoor large-scale sculpture such as *Eight American Sculptors* (1968) that John Henry had initiated in Chicago and in which Steve participated. After the lecture, Hall was asked if there had ever been an exhibition of large-scale outdoor sculpture off the pedestal. Yes, he said, but never in the Grand Rapids area.

Soon after this, the Women's Committee of GRAM asked Hall to consult on a sculpture show in downtown Grand Rapids. Hall recommended Steve, who visited the city to scout the site and probably talked with members of the Women's Committee. He also met Fred A. Myers, GRAM's new director, who had been recruited from the Carnegie Institute of Arts in Pittsburgh.[75]

Two years and $17,800 later, *Sculpture Off the Pedestal* opened.[76] Exhibiting artists were Stephen Antonakos, Mark di Suvero, Dale Eldred, Michael Hall, John Henry, William King, Lyman Kipp, John Mason, Clement Meadmore, Boyd Mefferd, Robert Morris, Robert Murray, and Steve.[77] Perfectly suited to spacious downtown Grand Rapids, *Sculpture Off the Pedestal* was a great success.

Steve showed *Arch,* which was probably the last piece that he made in the Lincoln Avenue studio. "The piece was in two parts," says Jerry Peart. "I welded it together and installed it in Grand Rapids. In those days, I was just learning how to work with aluminum."[78]

According to Peart, Steve raised money for his move to New York by sawing aluminum billet to transform it into sculpture. Some of these sculptures were complex: Steve worked out the designs in drawings, welded them together, and finished them. Others, which have been called "puzzle pieces," were made of multiple nested shapes. These were completely intuitive and easier to make. "In one month," says Peart, "Steve sawed out 15."[79]

Peart has both pleasant and uncomfortable memories of Steve. At one point, he built three small sculptures that Steve liked so much that he invited three Chicago dealers to the studio for a look. The dealers so respected Steve's judgment that two of them came to the studio. Walter Kelly took the sculptures on consignment, found buyers for them, and later gave Peart a show. "This is what Steve could do for people when he wanted to," Peart said.

"Steve was always depressed, always fighting that," Peart continued. "Everybody drank too much in those days and some did drugs." He added that Steve was much too willing to let others take care of him.[80]

In late spring of 1973, Steve and Michelle left for New York. As Zanzi remembers it, "we helped him load a tractor-trailer and he drove off into the night. It was a sad way to end his years in Chicago."[81]

Arch, 1973. Welded aluminum painted white, 21 ft. high. Permanently installed in Muskegon, Michigan. Photography by *Muskegan Chronicle* used by permission.

[1] The author had telephone conversations with Dolores Thurlby in August 2010 and on July 3 and October 7, 2011.

[2] Dolores explained that nudism "is beautiful because it brings together every age with no clothes on. You get in touch with people and you communicate. You're not looking at the jewelry, you're not looking at their bodies. It's like a direct leap to the soul with the eyes."

[3] Phone conversations with Dolores Thurlby.

[4] http://en.wikipedia.org/wiki/Lorado_Taft_Midway_Studios. The author visited the studios October 13, 2011.

[5] Phone conversations with Dolores Thurlby.

[6] Steve Urry lists the Midway Studios exhibitions on his two-page resume.

[7] E-mail correspondence with Peter Holbrook in 2011.

[8] They lived behind 846 W. Altgeld Street in a coach house that still stands. According to Brian Boyer's feature article "Up from Chicago: How a Nice Young Sculptor Crashed New York," *Chicago Tribune* (April 3, 1968), p. H36. Steve had a mustache when he lived on Altgeld Street, but shaved it off. The mustache collected aluminum dust and when it touched a filling, the pain took the top off Steve's head. According to Peter Holbrook, the Altgeld Street household was "a mess. I once saw Steve throw a plate of food at his TV—probably a war report or a political speech . . . Steve and Sprite took good care of their family in their crazy way." He adds that Steve "always got the latest tools—he introduced me to arc welding, spray painting, and strobe lights among other technologies. I'd say tools were probably the biggest household expense."

[9] http://en.wikipedia.org/wiki/Biograph_Theater.

[10] Larry Edwards, a now-retired Chicago lawyer and real estate investor, provided measurements of the studio. During 1973, Steve's last year in Chicago, Edwards purchased the building from its owner, a savings and loan association executive. Edwards wanted to run a movie theater, which he did for 12 years—and he says that he had "a lot of fun with it." In 2004, Edwards sold the building to Victory Gardens Theater, which transformed the interior into two live theaters. The upstairs where Steve had his studio now houses a rehearsal space and a studio theater. Telephone conversation with Larry Edwards, July 11, 2011.

Janis Urry recalls that Bob Silverman nicknamed Steve "Pig Pen" after the cartoon character because he was always so dusty and dirty from working in his studio. Lynn Urry says that Steve got to be friends with the pre-Edwards operator of the Biograph Theater who complained that business was slow. Steve suggested that he show art films, by which he meant films out of mainstream taste that often come from Europe. The theater owner thought that Steve wanted sex films and he started showing soft core pornography. Business boomed and Steve was declared a genius!

[11] Phone conversations with Dolores Thurlby.

[12] "I was the one who took care of Jeb all the time," she says. "Steve interacted with Jeb in the studio a little bit ... I did things like taking him to the zoo." Phone conversations with Dolores Thurlby.

[13] According to Lindy Bergman, widow of Edwin Bergman, the couple once had a sculpture by Steve in a house they owned in Lake Geneva, Wisconsin. The sculpture looked like three helmets. When they sold the house, the gardener took this piece, turned it upside down, and put plants in it. She has no idea where it is today. Conversation with Lindy Bergman, September 16, 2010.

[14] Vaughan Kurtz phone conversation, May 17, 2011.

[15] Interview with Ted Garner, May 19, 2011.

[16] Donald James Anderson. "Urry 'Dribblescapes' Bump and Burp Sculpture," *Chicago Magazine* (May-June 1971), pp. 7-9.

[17] *Mini Blatt* and *Shimi Blatt* were consigned to the Phyllis Kind Gallery, Chicago, on June 11, 1971, and shown by her after November 12, 1971.

[18] The Museum of Outdoor Arts, Englewood, Colorado, owns the cast welded aluminum *Psychedilly Rose II* (1968-1969), which is related visually to *Head Flower*. The sculpture is on permanent display at the museum. *Psychedilly Rose II* may originally have been conceived as a hanging sculpture; there is a photograph showing it suspended upside down. *Psychedilly Rose II* is exhibited at ground level at the Museum of Outdoor Arts with an extension at the left (actually a casting sprue, says Zanzi) that is elevated on a block of wood for balance.

[19] Dona Z. Meilach and Don Seiden, *Direct Metal Sculpture: Creative Techniques and Appreciation* (New York: Crown Publishers, 1966), pp. 100-02. Now retired, Seiden was a long-time sculpture instructor at the School of the Art Institute of Chicago. In a telephone conversation, he stated that he sent out lots of queries and Steve responded. Seiden never taught Steve. He started at SAIC in 1963, long after Steve was gone.

[20] Interviews with James Zanzi, April 4 and April 23, 2011.Steve and Zanzi probably met in 1965 and both exhibited at the Dell Gallery. Zanzi says that San Francisco was "overwhelmingly important" to Steve . It was "Steve's Ground Zero, the place where he got his basic attitudes." Steve made many castings for his sculptures at the School of the Art Institute of Chicago. He carved a form in Styrofoam, turned it upside down, embedded it in chemically-bonded sand, and poured in molten aluminum, which vaporized the foam and filled the cavity. At one point, instead of discarding the conical sprue that was formed when he poured aluminum into a sand mold, Steve used it in *Psychedilly Rose II*. Steve also made castings at a foundry operated by John Henry and probably in other locations as well. Steve made some lost wax castings and left waxes behind at Chicago's Sedgwick Studios where he worked in the 1980s. Steve's son Caleb has a white refractory casting shell that Steve apparently left behind when he departed his New York studio on Wooster Street in 1981.

[21] Phone conversations with Dolores Thurlby.

[22] Interview with Ellen Lanyon, April 18, 2011.Lanyon has given her archives to the Chicago Museum of Contemporary Art library where the author consulted them.

[23] Franz Schulze, "Some Final Thoughts about Phalanx 3," *Daily News* Panorama (December 18, 1965), p. 17; Joshua Kind, "Art News From Chicago," *Art News*, vol. 64, no.10, (February 1966), p. 46.

[24] Black and white photographs of *Spring Bubble* were published in the *Chicago Sun-Times* (May 15, 1966), and *Hyde Park Herald* (May 11, 1966).

[25] The corkscrewing arch piece was the subject of a cartoon in *Art Scene* (Chicago) vol. 1, no. 1, p. 21.

[26] Harold Hayden, "Showcase," *Chicago Sun-Times* (November 20, 1966), p. 7.

[27] *John Henry* (New York: Ruder Finn Press, 2010), p. 18, p. 34.

[28] "National Arts Council Announces Awards" *Chicago Tribune* (December 20, 1966), p. B1.; Thurlby phone conversations.

[29] E-mail correspondence with Stan Edwards, who supplied visuals.

[30] Holbrook e-mail correspondence.

[31] After reading a draft of this book, Peter Holbrook wrote (January 14, 2012): "What Steve was really about was the sculpture—that was the foundation of our relationship, along with many shared experiences and the fact that our ladies were good friends as well. ... I spent many days happily assisting Steve at work. I remember helping him wrestle a 500-pound arc welder up the stairs at the Altgeld [Street] coach house studio. He was very strong; I was too – which was a factor in our survival in those years."

[32] Royal Marks (1927-1987) opened his New York art gallery in 1962, specializing in modern American sculpture, primitives, and 20th century South American art.

[33] Holbrook e-mail correspondence.

[34] Brian D. Boyer, "Up from Chicago: How a Nice Young Sculptor Crashed New York," *Chicago Tribune* (April 21, 1968), p. H36. Amusing account of Urry's first New York show at Royal Marks Gallery—making the work in Chicago, truck trip to New York, and adventures there. A brief teaser extract from this article appears in the *Chicago Tribune* (April 21, 1968), p. F4.

[35] The drawings are in the collection of the Art Institute of Chicago and were examined there. Lynn Urry finds "a strange sphere" on top of *Questing Scape Study #6*. According to him, Steve liked "to put something that didn't belong on one of his shapes. How can you tell that something doesn't belong? After all, the shape is abstract. You have never seen anything like it and yet you have a strong feeling that something shouldn't be there, that something isn't quite right. He did justify it partly by putting a small spherical shape at the base of the form but it still seems out of place." Lynn adds: "I was at his loft in Chicago when a prospective customer liked a small piece, took it home, and after much thinking about it, came back and requested that a small awkward appendage be removed. Steve wouldn't do it."

[36] Boyer. *op. cit.*

[37] Not true. Steve showed *Psychedilly Rose* several times after 1967 and his son Caleb still owns parts of it. In 1978, Steve was involved in a lawsuit and had to list his major exhibitions and sales so his work could be evaluated. In this document, which is described in the next chapter, Steve stated that only three sculptures were sold from the *Ribbon Farm* show.

[38] Titles like *Psychedilly Rose* and *Head Flower* nod to the Hippie-LSD culture of the time. *Waul Phaulderawl* is a comic punning title like many that the Chicago Imagist painters gave to their work.

[39] Max Kozloff. *Artforum*, vol. 6 (December 1967), pp. 52-53; *Art in America*, vol. 55 (September 1967), p. 110; Grace Glueck. *New York Times* (October 29, 1967), p. 35.

[40] Interviews with James Zanzi. Zanzi said that he and Steve drove out to visit Royal Marks in November of 1967.They started out early in the morning and Steve drove until he surrendered the wheel to Zanzi because he wanted to get high. He was zonked out in the back seat the rest of the way. They arrived in New York just after the Royal Marks show came down and visited the dealer in his apartment, which he shared with his mother who berated him constantly. Royal Marks apologized for this, explaining that she was, after all, his mother! Later they delivered three of Steve's sculptures to an estate on Long Island (Zanzi cannot remember the owner's name), but were delayed when Steve picked up a waitress in a Greenwich Village blues club and spent the next three days with her. "When Steve disappeared from his household," says Zanzi, "it was often for romps like this."

[41] Jane Allen and Derek Guthrie, "Interview with Three Chicago Sculptors," *New Art Examiner*, vol. 4 (November 1976), p. 2. The three sculptors were Henry, Jerry Peart, and Barry Tinsley.

[42] E-mail correspondence with Michael Hall.

[43] Jane Allen and Derek Guthrie, "Interview"; *John Henry*.

[44] Interview with John Henry, June 21, 2010.

[45] Interview with Richard Hunt, April 4, 2011.Despite some similarities between their work, Hunt does not believe that he influenced Steve. Hunt said that Steve's work was influenced by his years in San Francisco—and by Robert Hudson and Alvin Light.

[46] Interviews with James Zanzi.

[47] Interview with Michael Hall.

[48] Photographs of the maquette for *Flower Power/Erection/Resurrection* are owned by the Urry family. Caleb Urry owns the correspondence with Loyola and the lawyers. James L. Reidy in *Chicago Sculpture* (Urbana, Illinois: University of Illinois Press, 1981), pp. 150-52, and Alice Sinkevitch in *American Institute of Architects Guide to Chicago* (New York: Harcourt Brace & Company, 1993), pp. 234-35, describe the sculpture and the controversy.

[49] *Dribblescapes* press materials from the Museum of Contemporary Art, Chicago. In the press release, Steve is quoted as stating that he began to make sculpture in art school. "The big attraction was to metal," he said. "I like hard, physical work and working with metal is certainly that."

[50] Conversations with John Adduci, Tom Scarff, August 3, 2010 and December 2, 2011.

[51] Conversation with Dan Blue, November 15, 2011.

[52] Franz Schulze, *Chicago Daily News* (July 26, 1969), p. 9.

[53] Franz Schulze, *Fantastic Images: Chicago Art Since 1945* (Chicago: Follett Publishing Co., 1972).

[54] Conversation with Franz Schulze, March 30, 2011.

[55] Steve gets perfunctory treatment in *Zabriskie: Fifty Years* (New York: Ruder Finn Press, 2010). The book documents Steve's

shows in 1969, 1972, and 1976, but provides no photographs or commentary. Zabriskie made small changes to the names of some sculptures from the *Dribblescapes* exhibition.

[56] *Time Magazine* (November 7, 1969); *Art News,* vol. 68 (December 1969), p. 72.

[57] Jane Allen and Derek Guthrie, "New City Plazas Provide Vistas for Forgotten Sculptors," *Chicago Tribune* (September 10, 1972), p. M22. Steve is quoted as saying, "It is too much trouble and expense to take large works to exhibitions unless they are commissioned first. I've never sold a piece from such a situation." This suggests one reason for Steve's change of scale.

[58] The author based these descriptions on photographs supplied by the Urry family and institutions such as the Smithsonian American Art Museum.

[59] Steve finished the surfaces of his "winged things" with an air-driven rotary brush that had a conical tip. On this tip were layers of sandpaper that wore off as he worked—and then were replaced by layers beneath. The result was long grooves on the metal surface that captured and scattered the light.

[60] Conversation with Claire Prussian, June 20, 2011.

[61] Conversation with Pamela Popeil August 5, 2011; *"Isn't That Amazing! The Appeal and Spiel of Ronco and Popeil"* Handout for a show at the Chicago Cultural Center, March 6 - May 16, 2004; "Clarence W. Thomas, "It Chops, It Slices, It Dices," *Journal of Popular Film and Television* (Summer 1989), pp. 67-73.

[62] Steve polished the cloud in this piece (and many others) with a mechanically driven rotating bristled brush (Flex-Shaft). According to studio-mates, he spent many hours polishing his sculptures, going into every corner.

[63] www.phylliskindgallery.com; Interview with Michael Hall.

[64] Jane Allen and Derek Guthrie, "Art: Second City Sculpture," *Chicago Tribune* (December 12, 1971), K22.

[65] Promotional Material from the Zabriskie Gallery, 1972.

[66] David L. Shirey, *Arts Magazine,* no. 46 (March 1972), p. 69; *New York Times* (February 26, 1972).

[67] Franz Schulze, *Chicago Imagist Art* (Exhibition Catalog), Chicago: Museum of Contemporary Art, 1972.

[68] Dennis Adrian. "Let's Show Off More Sculpture Downtown Like Steve Urry's," *Chicago Daily News Panorama* (September 9-10, 1972). Adrian also comments on Steve in "Aspects of Form among Chicago Artists," an essay reprinted in *Sight Out of Mind: Essays and Criticism on Art* (Ann Arbor: UMI Press, 1985). In this essay, he groups Steve with Chicago artists Jordan Davies, David Sharpe, Ed Flood, Suellen Rocca, Barbara Rossi, Karl Wirsum, Roger Brown, Jim Nutt, and Gladys Nilsson. "The interpretive history of art," he writes, "is largely, but by no means exclusively, the history of the development of forms rather than of subjects, and this is very much the case with a great deal of contemporary art where the form and/or material is the subject." He cautions that the artists he names are not members of some formal group and may not be familiar with each other's work. Still, they share a "common set of formal ideas."

In an interview on March 6, 2011, Adrian said that he met Steve a few times and that "we would talk about practical things like what's going into what show, can I see you later. He wasn't a big talker—to me at least." He added that Steve was "moody. . . he had a kind of interiority that one felt but did not have access to." Adrian did not like Michelle, whom Steve married in 1970. "She was too aggressive and wrecked his career," he said. "She had her gifts and accomplishments but I was not in a position to appreciate them."

[69] Thurlby phone conversations. According to Sprite, "When [Steve] started doing the sculptures, that's when I believe that our relationship started to slide." If Sprite and Steve met Michelle Altman in November of 1966 and the Altmans did not divorce until August of 1969, this suggests that the Altmans were separated for at least two years before they divorced. Obituaries of Michelle (see note 64 below) state that the Altman marriage lasted about a year. According to family sources, this marriage was never consummated.

[70] "Michelle Urry, R.I.P.," "www.sequential.spiltink.org/2006_10_01_archive.html; "Amidst an Ocean of T&A, She brought the Funny: Michelle Urry (1939-2006)," www.bunchness.blogspot.com/2006/10/amidst-ocean-of-t-she-brought-funny.html; "She Finds Entertainment for Men a Good Life," *New Woman* (September - October 1973), pp. 31-35; Interview with Janis Urry, May 26, 2011; E-mail from Peter Bradshaw, 2011.

[71] E-mail from Peter Bradshaw, September 13, 2010. The vinyl tubing seen in Bradshaw's photographs suggests that Steve had begun to work with this material in 1971. Mary Baber photographed Steve during 1971, probably during the summer, because the windows are open and he's lightly dressed. The vinyl hangings and a small inflatable sculpture are visible in the living area. On December 16, 1971, Michelle wrote to Virginia Zabriskie that Steve "has been getting tired of doing small perfect jewel-like pieces . . . and is longing to do something big. Somebody recently asked him to submit a drawing for a very large cloud to completely cover the ceiling of a room, and maybe that will satisfy his longing." In September of 1973, Steve exhibited a room-sized inflatable sculpture of clear plastic at the Virginia Zabriskie Gallery.

[72] Interview with Janis Urry.

[73] Interview with Jerry Peart, June 29, 2010, and e-mail correspondence during 2011.

[74] Archives of American Art, *Oral History Interview with Michael Hall,* July 19-26, 1976.

[75] David Cooper, "New Sculpture New Image: Grand Rapids' Grand Awakening," *Detroit Free Press,* November 18, 1973. It was probably through Myers that Steve made the contacts at Carnegie-Mellon that led to his visiting professorship and commission in 1974-1975.

[76] This was a very little money to stage such an ambitious show. Once the show was approved, the Women's Committee solicited cash and in-kind contributions from local businesses and individuals. The artists were given free room and board during their stay in Grand Rapids. Mary Ann Keeler was Treasurer of the show whose actual cost exceeded $130,000. Mary Ann Keeler, *Report on the "Sculpture Off the Pedestal" Show – 13 Sculptures* (produced for the Women's Committee of the Grand Rapids Art Museum), December 14, 1981.

[77] *Sculpture Off the Pedestal* exhibition catalog prepared by the Grand Rapids Art Museum. Grand Rapids, Michigan, Grand Rapids Art Museum, 1973.

[78] Interview with Jerry Peart.

[79] Steve began to make the sawed pieces before spring or summer of 1971, because Mary Baber photographed him in his studio at that time with many sawed pieces and sawed forms on the floor. During the 1980s, Steve lived in the Sedgwick Studios with John Adduci and Tom Scarff. While there, he made more sawed pieces, "using a band saw to cut aluminum in ways that it was never intended to be cut," says Adduci. "To make the sculptures, he had lubricant coming down the blade. He also used beeswax in cutting out the puzzle pieces. He never bent anything," Adduci adds, "but simply cut the billet into the shapes he wanted, using the inside piece as part of the puzzle." Interviews with Adduci, Scarff.

[80] Interview with Jerry Peart.

[81] Interviews with James Zanzi. According to Zanzi, Steve took marijuana, mescaline, and LSD. "On 10-day funks, he would lock himself in his studio and refuse to answer the door or telephone." Zanzi still has "great regard" for Steve as an artist. "He was a close friend who had a magic," he says. "Drinking I could handle, but heavy psychedelics began to control his life, causing a metamorphosis of his work and creating insurmountable problems for us. I lost patience with Steve and we had a final falling-out." Peter Holbrook has written that "Drugs were everywhere in those days—and not worth commenting upon."

NEW YORK AND AFTER

Untitled (For John). Signed "Urry 82" 1982.
Three-piece cast and sawed aluminum sculpture
whose elements fit together. Lightning bolt shape,
4¼ x 2 x 1¼ in; Small cast arch 6½ x 2¼ x 1¼ in;
Flat-topped sawed arch, 6½ x 2 ½ x 2 in.
Collection of John Adduci. Photo by Steve Greiner.

During the eight years that Steve lived in New York—1973 to 1981—his career advanced, peaked in 1976-77 with solo museum shows in Muskegon and Grand Rapids, Michigan—and then collapsed. In 1977, he lost a year's work when his sculptures were destroyed in transit. A lawsuit and settlement followed, but they could not bring back the work.

The Phyllis Kind Gallery dropped him before he left Chicago because he could not deliver work when needed. He was given a solo exhibit at the Zabriskie Gallery in New York in 1976, but that connection also ended. For a time in the 1970s, he was represented by Richard Friedman Fine Art Consultants, Chicago, but he had no subsequent dealers. During his New York years, Steve was in eight group exhibitions vs. 18 when he lived in Chicago. Most of these exhibits were in the Midwest with none in New York.

Critics reviewed Steve's Zabriskie show, but mostly he got news coverage after that. He made presentations and completed a commission at Pittsburgh's Carnegie-Mellon University during 1974-75 and won a big commission from the Nebraska I-80 Bicentennial Sculpture Project in 1975, but he did not complete that sculpture.

Steve lost his professional and social support system when he relocated. New York has no community of direct metal sculptors comparable to the community in Chicago. Since many New York sculptors design their work and have it fabricated elsewhere, Steve looked to Chicago for help when technical problems arose. The Hyde Park Urrys, who had provided so much encouragement and companionship in Chicago, were now 800 miles away—and his brother Lynn, to whom Steve was closest, lived in California.

Michelle supported Steve in New York and pressed him to decorate the living areas of their loft, care for their child, and accompany her to social events. These demands were reasonable, especially since he was earning so little, but women had always served Steve before—and he had walked away from his children. No surprise then, that personal relations between this mismatched pair were on-again, off-again. As often as not, he slept in his studio while Michelle occupied the living areas of their loft on the other side of a wall.

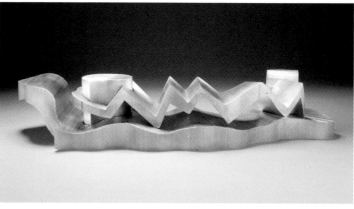

Untitled (Reclining Figure), ca. 1973.
Sawed aluminum, 3 x 17 x 8½ in.
Collection of Mary Ann Keeler, Grand Rapids.

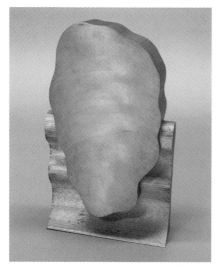

Untitled (Cloud Formations), 1973. Aluminum,
14¼ x 8⅝ x 3 (top) in. Collection of the Grand
Rapids Art Museum. Gift of Conrad and Molly
Bradshaw, 2004.17.

Grand Rapids; Muskegon

Soon after they moved into a 6,000-square-foot loft on New York's Wooster Street, Steve and Michelle departed to spend the summer in Europe. When they returned, Steve traveled to Grand Rapids for the September 8 opening of *Sculpture Off the Pedestal* where he and the other artists (listed in the previous chapter) received keys to the city.[1]

The Grand Rapids Art Museum (GRAM) led tours of *Sculpture Off the Pedestal*, providing docents with written statements from the exhibiting artists. In his statement, Steve called his entry, *Arch*, "a baroque, romantic piece," a "primordial symbol" like a rainbow. *Arch* "sets up a process of self-completion," he wrote, "as the bottom edges seem buried in the earth from which they appear to draw energy up one side, around the arch, and back down the other side . . . When in the center under the arch, an observer becomes balanced or 'charged' between the polar energy generated by the two sides."[2]

Separately, GRAM wrote that *Arch* was composed of "fantasy pieces of welded aluminum, cut-out jig-saw pieces." *Arch* was sited next to an office building to protect it from the wind. The "shadow of the piece moves with the light across the background of the buildings," said GRAM.[3]

Steve returned several times to the Grand Rapids area between 1973 and 1977, connecting with influential people as he showed and sold his work. Mary Ann Keeler, a founder and financial backer of GRAM, played a prominent role in organizing and financing *Sculpture Off the Pedestal*. She purchased a sculpture from Steve and helped him to sell his work in the Grand Rapids area.

For years, Keeler had collected art with her industrialist husband, buying "by our eyes," as she put it, instead of letting dealers tell them what to do. The Keelers had excellent eyes! Their home is filled with first-class contemporary art including works by Picasso, di Suvero, and Steve's untitled aluminum puzzle piece, which Keeler purchased directly from him and christened *Reclining Figure*. The "figure" in this 3- x 17- x 8-inch sculpture is a jagged saw-cut piece of aluminum billet that lies atop the body of the sculpture like someone in bed.[4]

Keeler helped Steve sell *Arch* to the City of Muskegon, Michigan, which is 42 miles northwest of Grand Rapids. When *Sculpture Off the Pedestal* came down in December, *Arch* stayed in the area for about a year. On November 13, 1974, the *Muskegon Chronicle* reported that the Mayor of the city had "broached the idea (of purchase) to the City Commission."[5]

By this time, the National Endowment for the Arts had offered to provide matching funds for half the $13,000 price if Muskegon could come up with the other half. Some locals opposed the purchase, calling *Arch* a colossal lasagna and "the Jolly Green Giant's urinal."

Declaring that times were hard and that "there was not enough money for leaf raking," the Muskegon City Commission voted 5-2 against purchasing *Arch*. Then, Robert D. Swedenberg, a Muskegon physician, declared his intention to supply $6,500 toward the sculpture. He wanted to give it to Muskegon in memory of his wife and as a memorial from her family members.

The next vote was unanimous in favor of the piece. By February of 1975, a lakefront site was under consideration. Soon after that, *Arch* was installed and dedicated with Steve present. Today it remains Steve's only surviving large-scale public sculpture.[6]

Carnegie-Mellon

For half a semester during the fourth quarter of 1974, Steve was visiting Andrew Mellon professor of sculpture at Carnegie-Mellon University in Pittsburgh. While there, he learned that David M. Schmid had given stainless steel sheets to the art department for use by sculpture students. Schmid, a Carnegie-Mellon graduate, was founder, Board chairman, and treasurer of the Techalloy Company in Rahns, Pennsylvania, which manufactured stainless steel and nickel products.

Steve decided to make a stainless steel sculpture, but he lacked equipment to cut the metal, found nothing satisfactory in Pittsburgh, and finally got what he needed from Chicago. Once he started work, he recruited his students to build the sculpture and introduced them, gleefully no doubt, to the Steve Urry lifestyle.

"The students have been wonderful," he told the *Pittsburgh Post-Gazette*. "Rather than follow a set time for classes, they come and go at all hours and we frequently work all night. Afterwards I stumble to my bed in my studio here and the next thing I know, it's midday. . . . We've been eating, living, and breathing sculpture." Even with all this help, fabrication took longer than expected, and Steve had to move the work off campus to a space provided by a local steel company.

When *Reflections* was installed during August 1975, Donald Miller, art critic of the *Pittsburgh Post-Gazette*, described it as "mainly minimal in style . . . a large ribbon of asymmetric planes that arches above the earth on three graceful points. It is about eight feet tall, weighs 6,000 pounds, and is semicircular. One end is on the ground; the other cantilevers like an arm beckoning one to the center."

"For an abstract, the sculpture is unusually inviting," Miller continued. "A small person may crawl through its hollow length. This offers a different tangent for so severe a style which we tend to think of as an aloof entity."[7]

Steve explained to *Carnegie Alumni News* that *Reflections* "takes on a sort of organic movement, arching into space and twisting and turning for some 30 feet to create a lot of tension and a transition from a massive to a more ethereal feeling with Gothic geometrical severity." He added that *Reflections* was highly polished both inside and out so "its angular facets will reflect each other, multiplying infinitely to create a striking aesthetic effect. . . . A climb through it should be as fascinating as its exterior, which will mirror its surroundings: the sky, the grass and trees, and the people passing by." He knew of no other sculpture that rewards viewing both inside and outside.

"Working with stainless steel is very real physical labor," Steve continued. "It is such a hard metal and the sheets are so heavy, you must have a crane to lift them into place. It's difficult to weld or cut without very special equipment, but it is wonderful to work with. It's beautiful for the geometry that can be created; it can't be bent but it can be smoothed or rounded; and it holds its polish forever."[8]

Reflections, Steve's only piece in stainless steel, is strikingly different from his other sculptures in part because he could not work as freely with stainless as with aluminum or steel. *Reflections* recalls two geometric steel-rod constructions that Steve welded together in the Wooster Street loft. He may have been experimenting with those ideas before he went to Carnegie-Mellon or he may have brought them back with him.

Reflections is destroyed. According to Lynn Urry, Steve told him that "one night, a

Steve Urry, David Schmid, and student at Carnegie-Mellon University with *Reflections* under construction, 1975.

Reflections, 1975. 15 x 40 x 5 ft. (destroyed). Installed on Carnegie-Mellon campus, Pittsburgh, Pennsylvania.

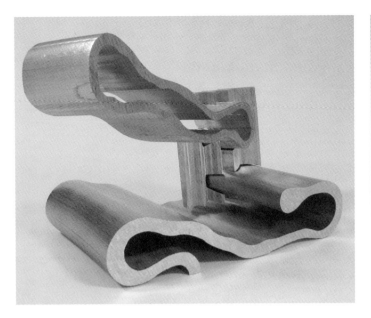
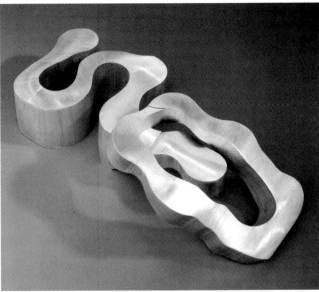

Untitled Maquette, 1976. Aluminum,
10 x 13¼ x 10¾ in. Collection of the Muskegon
Museum of Art. Hackley Picture Fund Purchase,
1977.2.

Untitled (O-shape and long S-shape), signed
"S. Urry 1973," sawed aluminum S-Form,
12¼ x 6 x 3 in.; (O-Form), 10 x 6¼ x 2¼ in.
Collection of Dawn Clark Netsch, Chicago.
Photo by Steve Greiner.

group of well-oiled fraternity brothers climbed on top of the piece and began to bounce up and down on it at its resonant frequency. This type of activity can bring down the strongest of structures. In the military, soldiers are required to break cadence when crossing bridges in order to keep from exciting the bridge's resonant frequency and bringing it down. Steve said that the piece was extensively reinforced and he couldn't believe they could produce so much damage."[9]

David L. Beck

Steve's assistant as he fabricated *Reflections* was David L. Beck, a Carnegie-Mellon student who is today a well-known San Francisco sculptor. After graduation in 1976, Beck moved to New York and lived for about two years in the Wooster Street loft. Steve and Michelle had a full floor, one-third of which was living space that Steve had "fixed up very nicely," says Beck, and the remainder was studio. The two men slept in the studio most of the time. At one point, Michelle purchased a small weekend house in Sag Harbor at the eastern end of Long Island.

According to Beck, Steve made aluminum sculptures at Wooster Street, which Beck calls "cut pieces." These were thick squares of aluminum with the center shallowly cut in a spiral and then pulled up at the end to create a tape-like form that spiraled gently upward. These pieces were apparently exhibited at the Zabriskie Gallery and a "cut piece" was used in a cigarette ad to suggest floating smoke.[10]

Steve made a sauna in the studio from cardboard washing machine and refrigerator boxes that he fitted together in the shape of an L. Every morning, he would go inside, spray water on the coils of an electric heater there to make steam, sit for awhile, jump up, and run to the shower.

Caleb Urry, Steve and Michelle's son, was born on January 22, 1976, and Beck became his babysitter. When Beck got his own studio and moved out, Steve would visit him with Caleb in tow. Beck says that Steve was very devoted to Caleb.

Nebraska Commission

In the fall of 1970, Steve exhibited *Psychedilly Rose* in *American Sculpture: An Exhibition Organized to Inaugurate the Sheldon Sculpture Garden at the University of Nebraska, Lincoln.* Organized by Norman Geske, director of the Sheldon Museum, the show was a complete survey of the history of American sculpture. It comprised 174 works by artists ranging from Augustus Saint-Gaudens and Horatio Greenough to Alexander Calder, David Smith, Michael Hall, and Steve. *Psychedilly Rose* was published in the show catalog.

Steve probably visited Lincoln for the opening of this important show and met Norman Geske who became a very valuable contact. By 1973, Geske was involved with the Nebraska I-80 Bicentennial Sculpture Project, which commissioned 10 large-scale outdoor sculptures at rest stops on both sides of Interstate Highway 80. Popularly called "Nebraska's 500-Mile Sculpture Garden," the project was scheduled for completion on July 4, 1976, to commemorate America's Bicentennial.

In February of 1974, the Bicentennial Sculpture Project solicited bids nationwide. One hundred and twenty-one artists responded. Of these, 38 were invited to submit final proposals. By March 5, Steve had reached the second round. In a letter to Geske, Urry thanked him for his interest in his work and proposed "an arch, 30 feet high, wide enough to be driven through by two cars," and enclosed a drawing. It would take " approximately six months" to fabricate such a sculpture in his New York studio, he stated. "In order to withstand the elements, the internal bracing job would be formidable, as complicated as an airplane wing." Steve estimated that he would need another three weeks to weld the sculpture together on site.[11]

"I have been thinking out the aesthetics of arches in small and large scale for some time," Steve continued, "and when I saw the sample [project] sites, it struck me that a giant redwood tree-sized arch might be perfect for Nebraska." Steve had other ideas if this highway-straddling arch was rejected.

The arch was rejected, but Steve won a commission for *Platte River Ribbon,* a 25 x 10 x 22 ft. aluminum sculpture that was designated for installation next to the Platte River in the eastbound Cozad rest area near the center of Nebraska. Steve's design (see page 50) was a ribbon-like form that started on the ground at left, curved upward and around, returned to the ground at right, and then made a second, smaller arch inside the larger one.

In his project narrative, Steve connected *Platte River Ribbon* to his childhood "first impressions" of Nebraska when the Urry family "often traveled cross-country" from the west coast to Chicago. "I remember the craggy mountains of Wyoming," he wrote, "which would be followed by more arid country where soft undulating shapes were punctuated only by sage. When we arrived on the plains of Nebraska, we always felt an hypnotic effect, produced by moving through the sunlit flatness of the prairies on an endless ribbon of road."

"We would stop to rest by the river for lunch," he continued, "and watch its mean-dering. Though the river submits completely to the contours of nature, the river rhythms seem to echo the man-made ribbons of the road." His concept, he stated, was "a sculptural rendition of a ribbon symbolizing the roads and rivers of Nebraska." Walking through his sculpture would be "a subtle condensation, intensifying the experience of physical motion [that one has while driving] within an artist's personal symbolic vision."

Platte River Ribbon recalled much that Steve had done in the past and anticipated his next body of work. The commission budget was apparently finalized on January 16, 1975, with $11,002.50 allowed for materials and $16,800.20 for Steve's work, making an estimated total of $27,802.70.

The I-80 project was a very public affair involving countless politicians and bureau-crats along with Nebraska citizens who voiced opinions in public meetings. On July 31, 1975, the *New York Times* reported that the project had raised "geysers of controversy." The criticisms "generally fall along these lines," said the *Times.* "The works, as depicted by scale models, either do not represent Nebraska or do so poorly; public funds are being squandered; none of the artists are Nebraskans; [and] the puzzling abstractions will give Nebraska a false reputation as people drive by the cross-state

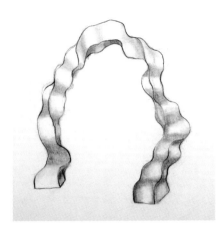

Untitled drawing of arch sculpture.
Signed "S. Urry 76." Pencil on paper, 13 x 10½ in.
Collection of S. Thomas Scarff.

Article in local Nebraska newspaper shows
Steve's final design for the Cozad sculpture.

sculpture garden in subsequent years."[12]

On July 3, 1975, possibly in response to such criticism, Nebraska Governor J. James Exon held back $150,000 in state funding for the I-80 project. This shrank the project budget, creating a shortfall that Project Director Art Thompson estimated at $228,600, a sum which Thompson hoped to raise from other sources.

On September 1, 1975, Steve said that he could start work by October and that it would take him eight months to fabricate the sculpture in his studio. Installation could begin in May 1976 and the piece would be up by deadline. Steve signed a contract on March 20, 1976. Porter Engineering of Lincoln, Nebraska prepared engineering drawings of *Platte River Ribbon* which were approved on May 18.

Meanwhile, plans were underway for a grand statewide dedication on July 4 with congressmen, VIPs, and television cameras present. In February, Steve said that he would not be ready by deadline. He received $6,000 or one-third of his commission on March 23. Soon after that, Steve apparently told the Project Director that he would need more money to complete the sculpture. On June 13, the Cozad Chamber of Commerce asked for $10,000 from the National Endowment for the Arts that apparently was not awarded. In late July, Steve, Michelle, and the infant Caleb visited Cozad where Steve made public presentations. He received $5,000—the second installment of his commission—on December 30. All along, the Project reimbursed Steve's material and travel expenses.

Eight of the 10 artists completed their sculptures and earned their commissions. On its website, the Sheldon Museum of Art states that Steve's sculpture was never completed "because of a major delay in the fundraising process necessitated by the legislature's decision to hold public hearings regarding acceptance of the sculptures."

Steve, in fact, never started the fabrication of *Platte River Ribbon*. According to David Beck, they purchased "a ton of aluminum sheet which we winched up to the second floor studio by removing the window." When the Nebraska project could no longer pay him, Steve invoked a clause in his contract stipulating the conditions under which he would not be required to finish the work. After that, he decided to dump the aluminum instead of making sculpture from it. After calling around to scrap dealers, he ended up taking pennies on the dollar.[13]

Clear Plastic Sculpture

Steve began to experiment with clear plastic sculpture in 1971 while he was still living in Chicago.[14] Plastic materials were easier to build with than metal and gave Steve new ways to explore his forms.

In September 1973, Steve showed *Sculpture for One Room,* a 144 x 420 x 120 in., room-sized inflatable sculpture at the Zabriskie Gallery. Writing in *Art News,* Michael Andre described this work as "an inflated sculpture of clear plastic [that] caterpillared its way about the rear gallery. There were three balloons and each averaged about two feet in diameter and 20 feet in length. Each of the balloons blipped and contracted like an elegant tree limb. The smallest balloon created a circle from floor to ceiling. The place was an environment that one stepped through and a sculptural triptych in the manner of Henry Moore."[15]

From this description—we have no photographs—we can imagine that *Sculpture for One Room* was a meandering intestinal form, larger in scale than those that Steve had made in metal and with a quite different feeling to it. Steve, the tireless experimenter, had found a fresh way to make art.

Jeremy Gilbert-Rolfe misread *Sculpture for One Room* in *Artforum* (December 1973). Instead of seeing it as something new, he connected it to superficial characteristics of Steve's sculpture and San Francisco and Chicago influences. "Steve Urry's work has become flabby and overconfident," Gilbert-Rolfe wrote. Urry's "background is

Chicago and San Francisco, and it shows . . . His plastic is heat-welded, and this gives an irregular contour to the sculpture suggestive of the funky look of the drawing in West Coast head comics."[16]

In March and April of 1974, Steve showed *Sculpture for One Room* in *Contemporary American Painting and Sculpture,* a group exhibition at the Krannert Art Museum, Champaign, Illinois. The show catalog published a photograph of a young woman looking at the piece, but she occupies the center of the picture and we only see parts of the sculpture at the edges.[17]

Polyurethane Sculpture

Steve began making polyurethane isocyanate resin sculpture in the Wooster Street studio. Polyurethane resins are used to make boats, piping, auto bodies, insulation, and much more. They are typically two-part systems—a resin and a curing agent—that are mixed prior to use. The curing agent or hardener contains isocyanates that act as a catalyst and help cure the resin to a hard plastic.[18]

According to Beck, Steve's first polyurethane isocyanate resin sculptures were crude. As his skills advanced and the work grew bigger, Steve built his sculptures with cardboard armatures. After putting the armature in place, he created the rough form of a piece by shaping blocks of hard plastic foam with a rasp and an electric carving knife.

He built with these blocks and then sprayed on polyurethane isocyanate foam using a machine that combined the resin and the curing agent to create foam. The foam came out of a gun that allowed Steve to control the flow and density of the foam. This process gave him such creative flexibility and spontaneity that he felt as if he were drawing in air.[19]

Once he finished spraying on the foam and letting it harden, Steve rasped and sanded the sculpture smooth, primed it, and applied a top coat of lacquer that he rubbed by hand. Making polyurethane sculptures was very hard work. Beck says that his and Steve's hands bled.[20]

In January 1976, Steve showed some of these expanded large-scale polyurethane isocyanate resin sculptures at the Zabriskie Gallery. This work was apparently photographed in the Wooster Street studio. On the left, a long, twisted, very lumpy intestinal sculpture that could be eight feet tall leans against the wall. In the back of the photograph is a tubular work, undulating and coiled in a circle, whose highest part reaches about seven feet up to the top of a window. This piece is intestinal, like Steve's clear plastic sculpture and some of the metal work he made in the late 1960s and early 1970s. Its meandering form recalls parts of *Double X* and other steel sculptures.

Three pieces in this show foreshadow Steve's December exhibition in Muskegon. In the right rear corner of the room is a spiral-form sculpture made from a sheet-like length of plastic. Steve apparently showed this work in Muskegon, calling it *Untitled #6.*

The other two pieces are free-standing vertical sculptures with bulbous lower parts and tubular upper parts. These forms are biomorphic, but do not read as any specific plant or animal. The sculpture closest to the viewer on the right consists of two parts joined together by a tubular arch-like form. Either or both of these pieces may have gone to Muskegon. It's difficult to make a positive identification from the photographs that we have.

Nancy Grove published a long, thoughtful review of the Zabriskie show in *Arts* (January 1976). "Urry makes no drawings for his pieces," she wrote, "though he may sketch on the forms as he works. The sculptures themselves are often like quick draw-ings or spontaneous gestures, particularly the expanded polyurethane pieces, which might be described as 'action sculpture.' Large bulging tubular shapes arc and twist freely into space, enclosing areas framed by subtly rippling edges. Surfaces are pitted and lumpy but light-reflecting, so that the piece reads both as undulating, unified form

Untitled preparatory drawing for polyurethane isocyanate resin sculpture. Signed "Urry 76". Pencil on paper, 11 x 14 in.

Untitled polyurethane isocyanate resin sculpture at Muskegon Museum of Art, 1976.

and as discrete textural variations."

She added that expanded polyurethane is used for roofing and insulation. "Sprayed as a foam, it expands and hardens to any desired density. It can be built up and carved into, giving the artist more immediate access to any imagined form." She adds that Urry is just beginning to explore this material "with results that convey a delightful sense of exuberance and freedom."[21]

Hackley Art Museum

In the 1870s and 1880s, Muskegon was the "Lumber Queen of the World" with 50 sawmills and much wealth, but the industry and the city fell on hard times in the 1890s. Instead of walking away from the stricken town, Charles H. Hackley, a wealthy lumberman, stayed on and worked to make Muskegon "one of the most distinctive cities of its size in the country,"as he put it. He gave money for a public library, a city park, a hospital, and much else, but died in 1905 before a projected art museum could be realized. In his will, Hackley left funds to purchase works of art, and the museum, named in his honor, went up in 1912. In 1975, the Hackley Museum changed its name to the Muskegon Museum of Art.[22]

On July 28, 1975, Shirley Howarth, director of the Hackley Museum, offered Steve a one-man show of "models and smaller sculptures" in the museum's center gallery. Steve, who had visited the Hackley, accepted the invitation, but asked for a later date because he was tied up with the Nebraska sculpture. Howarth visited the Wooster Street studio in late November, stating afterwards that "I was excited by your idea for your 'new medium'" (presumably polyurethane). In her letter, she enclosed a museum floor plan that seemed to anticipate a mixed show of "environmental work" and "smaller sculptures."[23]

The exhibition opened on December 3, 1976, with Steve showing 17 pencil sketches and five monumental polyurethane sculptures, all of which he had made that year. According to the Museum, "Urry has been experimenting with a new material, polyurethane isocyanate resin, which he feels is more versatile than aluminum."Steve declared that "the work should last forever . . . it's as strong as maple."These words would come back to haunt him.

Howarth apparently wrote the unsigned, undated account of Steve's show that survives in museum files. The document states that Urry already has *Arch* in Muskegon, but "I thought it would be helpful to see several of his works to get a better idea of what he is trying to accomplish. [Also to] see preliminary sketches which give insight into his process of creation."

[Steve is] "becoming more fluid,"the document continues. Polyurethane isocyanate resin "has allowed him to break away . . . to become 3-D and completely free, to get away from the technical problems which aluminum created. Now he can create any shape he wants without having to worry about bracing and balancing."This could very well summarize what Steve told Howarth when she visited his studio.

Steve drove 785 miles from New York to Muskegon for the opening, a "horrendous" trip that left him completely exhausted. According to the *Muskegon Chronicle,* his show was scheduled next for GRAM, then "Texas, San Francisco, Chicago, New York, and Los Angeles."The work traveled to GRAM in January, but the rest of this projected tour never happened.[24]

Steve's polyurethane isocyanate resin sculptures ranged in height from four to 11 feet; one was 20 feet wide. Monumental in form and intention, they recall his box-constructed aluminum sculptures from the mid-60s, except that the forms are looser because he was working in plastic. Since he could not grind or weld plastic, these sculptures are more unitary and less improvisational than his metal work.

The most ambitious and successful pieces in the Muskegon/GRAM shows were three tall, leaning arch-like forms made of a combination of flat, tape-like, and tubular shapes to suggest plant or animal life. Some elements in these sculptures look like castings, others recall bone, and one has a pelvis shape. Bud and puckering forms appear in these pieces as do tubular shapes that flatten out. The other two sculptures in the Hackley show were vessels with a sprayed surface and the tape-like spiral sculpture that he had shown at Zabriskie Gallery.[25]

A Devastating Loss

When the Hackley Museum show came down on January 2, 1977, the museum flew Steve to Muskegon, where he and Pat Carlson, a GRAM employee, packed the work in a truck, which was then driven roughly 50 miles to Grand Rapids for the second stop on its tour. Since Steve would not be in Grand Rapids when the GRAM show came down on February 1, Carlson was assigned to pack the work and arrange for its return to New York. He was assisted by Fred Myers, GRAM's director. Gray Sweeney, a Grand Rapids college art teacher, witnessed the work.[26]

The work was badly packed and it arrived severely damaged at Steve's studio. According to Lynn Urry, "Steve visited me right after the episode and described the whole thing. When Steve and the truck driver opened the back of the truck, Steve went into a state of shock.

"It was the truck driver who suggested to Steve that he sue the museum . . . [He] described the packing job and his description was confirmed by the document written by Pat Carlson. All of the pieces were wrapped in foam and placed on the floor of the truck . . . [they] were secured together by a rope holding them all down to the bed of the truck. This won't work! According to Steve, each piece was to be individually secured by its own rope. Had that been done, the shipment would have survived."

On February 2, Steve examined his work, photographed it, made drawings of some pieces, and typed out "A Summary of Damage and Repair" which stated that four of the five pieces were damaged beyond repair and estimated his loss at "$65,000 plus." The single piece that might be fixed is "priced at $20,000" he added, and "will take approximately $8,000 to $10,000 worth of work to bring it close to its original condition." He was not certain that he could repair this piece and stated that the damage sustained, and need for restoration cut its value in half.[27]

Later that year, to justify the dollar amount of his claim, Steve provided his lawyers with a 10-year list of major sales, a five-year list of minor sales, a summary of damage and repair to his sculptures, and documentation of his professional career. On June 29, in a letter to David Bartlett, who was probably another lawyer, M. David Distler, Steve's lawyer, stated that the "problem of valuation is both an interesting and complicated one."

"Mr. Urry is a well-known and recognized sculptor with impressive talents," he continued. "Although he is working in a new medium, the very fact that this medium requires an unusual amount of technical skill and training must add to the value of the pieces. There is no other known sculptor in the United States who is working in his medium." The lawyer concluded that Steve's work is "ultra-unique."[28]

The insurance company paid Steve $48,030 for the loss of his sculptures. For three years after that, lawyers for the insurance company, the Hackley Art Museum, and the trucking firm wrangled over who should pay what to whom. The story got into the newspapers which recalled Steve's earlier statements that his work was "hard as maple" and "would last forever."[29]

After this, Steve participated in two major group shows. The first was the catalogued *CHICAGO: The City and its Artists, 1945-1978* at the University of Michigan Museum of Art, Ann Arbor, from March 17 to April 23, 1978. Steve showed *Oop-Zig* from 1966. From February 12 to March 28, 1981, Steve's cast/welded aluminum *Untitled* (1970), which had been given to the Renwick Museum in 1980 by Samuel

Untitled drawing of knotted sculpture. Signed "Urry 76." 14 x 11 in.

Untitled (Double starburst piece, small starburst inside large), ca.1980s. Sawed aluminum, 7¾ x 9 x 3½ in. Collection of John Adduci. Photo by Steve Greiner.

Koffler, was exhibited in the cataloged *Recent Trends in Collecting: Twentieth Century Painting and Sculpture from the National Museum of American Art* at the National Museum of American Art, Washington, D.C.

Kim Del Giorno

During his years with Michelle and later, Steve had an off-again, on-again relationship with his daughter Kim Urry (Del Giorno) from his marriage to Gail Schwartz. According to Del Giorno, she was born in 1959 and last saw her father in 1962. When she was about 10 years old, he sent her an abstract sculpture whose shape she likens to a seal.

In 1978, when she was 18 and enrolled in a Los Angeles beauty school, Del Giorno telephoned Steve in New York City. Their first conversation was short and stilted, but then he called her back and they talked for two hours. After that they talked almost every day. She would come home expecting the call at a certain time and she welcomed this opportunity to get to know her father, feeling that they had much in common temperamentally. She reminded him of his sister Kay, Steve said.

The two made plans to meet in New York, but Steve suddenly fell silent. She called once, but the conversation was uncomfortable. She did not make the trip and imagines that Michelle had re-entered Steve's life. Steve and Kim talked for the last time in 1993 when he was living in Tempe. Again they made plans to meet, but Steve's parents had not told her how sick he really was—and he was reluctant to have her see him because he had lost a great deal of weight. He died, and the family held the funeral before she could get to Tempe.[30]

In 1981, Steve and Michelle divorced and he left the Wooster Street studio. According to Dave Beck, the separation was amicable. Steve and Michelle joked about grounds for divorce, speculating on what "mental cruelty" might be.[31] John Henry sent a semi-trailer truck to New York, and Steve loaded it with his studio equipment, sculptures, and personal possessions. Then he went to live with Henry in Miami. Steve was 42 years old in 1981. His life was over but not yet ended.[32]

Miami; Chicago[33]

Chronology becomes vague at this point, and we see Steve in glimpses. Once he arrived in Miami, Steve apparently moved into a garage and expected to become John Henry's studio assistant. According to Janis Urry, Henry fired one of his studio assistants who came back into the building later and stole Steve's metal fabricating equipment. We do not know exactly when this happened. Steve's possessions were apparently not recovered.

Steve then returned to Chicago, bunked with his parents in Hyde Park, and commuted to the Sedgwick Studios where he assisted John Adduci, Tom Scarff, and Jerry Peart. The Sedgwick Studios are an industrial building on Chicago's north side and has served as residences and studios for large-scale metal sculptors for many years.

In 1982, Steve worked on two Scarff commissions, one of which was an eight-story hanging piece for General Motors in Detroit. He assisted with a Peart sculpture and apparently returned to Miami when that work was completed.

In 1985, Peart and Adduci sent for Steve to assist them with building Peart's 39-foot sculpture, *Blue Geisha*. Adduci remembers Steve as "completely self-absorbed" at this time. "He drank heavily and sometimes crashed at the studio after an evening at a local bar, rather than going to the home of his parents. He also smoked marijuana, but never took hard drugs."[34]

Steve moved into Adduci's house. "I had a wife and two young daughters then," Adduci recalls. "My house was a four-story building. I rented out the basement, which was below street level and located the bedrooms on the first floor so I could put my children straight out the windows in case of fire, instead of dropping them 10 feet.

We had the living room and kitchen on the second floor. Steve lived alone in the third-floor attic."

"Steve was obsessed with the I-Ching, the ancient Chinese book of divination, and filled notebooks with notations.[35] He paid no attention to my family and sometimes stayed in his room for days at a stretch. We all knew he was there. This arrangement gave my wife the willies and she wanted him gone, which he was after about a month."

Steve next moved into Adduci's studio office and lived there two years, but he finally had to leave because Adduci's clients would walk in to find him sleeping on the sofa. After that, he lived in a single room occupancy hotel nearby, using money from Michelle. Eventually, says Sedgwick sculptor Dan Blue, Steve's presence became problematic because there was no work for him.

The Sedgwick sculptors saw Steve daily and got to know him well. They observed that he was not very sophisticated about art. "He knew a little art history," says Scarff, "and knew his contemporaries, but he would not visit the Art Institute."

Steve would work like a madman for several days, stop cold, go into a depression, and do nothing. Sometimes he sat on a chair in a corner of the studio for hours, not moving or speaking. "He's in the position!" the sculptors would say. They concluded that he was bipolar and urged him to seek help, but he refused. John Henry had made similar suggestions in Miami.

At his best, Steve inspired the Sedgwick sculptors with his enthusiasm and uncanny making skills. They watched him cut out "puzzle pieces" like those he'd made in 1973 to finance his move to New York. He would step up to the band saw with aluminum billet in his hands, cut out the piece without stopping, do some light finishing, and be done.

"Steve *loved* to work!" says Blue. "He was possessed. Once you set him up, he was like a kid. A very sweet guy, he was never into money. Finances limited him from doing all he wanted to."

Blue recalls that a friend gave Steve a plasma cutter, which cuts metal much faster than the oxy-acetylene torches that he was using. The cutter was a 4-by-12-foot table equipped with an optical tracer that follows a drawing to guide the cutting torch. "Steve did plasma cutting free-lance," says Blue. "He'd pick up the electric eye on the cutter and use it to make crazy shapes in half-inch plate. He had the ability to conceive sculpturally and to come up with something coherent when he worked like this. Others might try the same thing, but they'd get garbage."

At the Sedgwick Studios, Steve also built painted aluminum constructions that recall Robert Hudson's work. He cut aluminum plate into flat shapes and strips which he twisted, bent, and welded into pedestal-sized works that incorporate some of his familiar forms—the leaning arch, "puckering" flower, and meandering ribbon. He painted these sculptures in bright shiny colors, but a careful look tells us that he never quite finished them.

One of the painted constructions is shield-like and decorated with colored encaustic in a mottled pattern. During his years at the Sedgwick Studios, Steve also began painting a large street scene with little cartoonish people, but the piece was never finished. These works, which never were exhibited, have been stored in Chicago since he left.

Steve knew that his career had tanked and blamed Michelle for using New York lawyers to file suit after his sculptures were destroyed. He claimed he was boycotted after that. Still, he kept in touch with Michelle and she sometimes sent him money. He does not seem to have had any other women in his life. A Chicago artist, who prefers to remain anonymous, remembers one or two promising dates with him in the 1980s, but he then he telephoned her to say that he was simply unable to pursue a relationship.

According to the Sedgwick Studio sculptors, Steve left Chicago for the last time in 1986 or 1987 and presumably went to Miami. In 1989, John Henry moved from Miami

Untitled (For John), 1982. Signed "Urry 82". Three-piece cast and sawed aluminum sculpture whose elements fit together. Lightning bolt shape, 4¼ x 2 x 1¼ in; small cast arch 6½ x 2¼ x 1¼ in; flat-topped sawed arch, 6½ x 2½ x 2 in. Collection of John Adduci. Photo by Steve Greiner.

Clockwise from top:
Untitled (Inset starburst and long cast form arching over top). ca. 1982. Cast/welded, sawed aluminum, 21 x 23 x 2¾ in. Collection of Janis Urry. Photo by Steve Greiner.

Untitled (Dan's Puzzle Piece), ca. 1982. Sawed aluminum, 16 x 4¼ x 3 in. (work not completed). Collection of Dan Blue. Photo by Steve Greiner.

Untitled (Three-piece sculpture with flat plate, block, and constructed tunnel form), ca. 1982. Cast and welded, sawed aluminum, 11¾ x 8 x 8¾ in. Outer portion: 8¼ x 9 x 3¾ in; inner portion: 4¼ x 6½ x 3¼ in. Collection of Janis Urry. Photo by Steve Greiner.

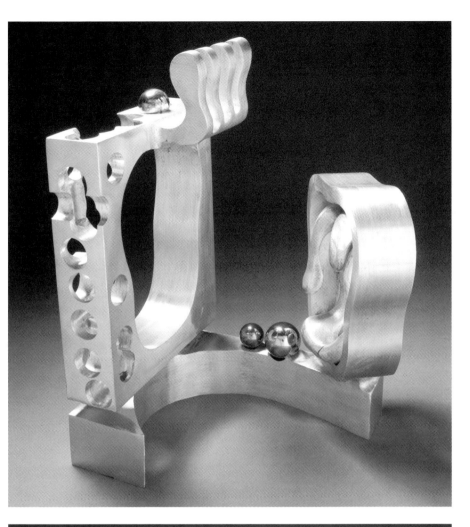

Untitled (Cut piece with multiple holes and steel balls), ca. 1982. Cast/welded/sawed aluminum, steel, 12½ x 8 x 6¾ in. Collection of John Adduci. Photo by Steve Greiner.

Untitled (Three-part piece with pins and holes. At left are two stacked semicircles; middle is two-walled piece with tops joined, large hole in center; right is three finger-like forms), ca. 1980s. Cut, formed aluminum, 7½ x 9½ x 9 in. Collection of Dan Blue. Photo by Steve Greiner.

 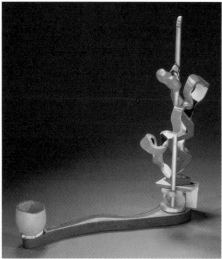 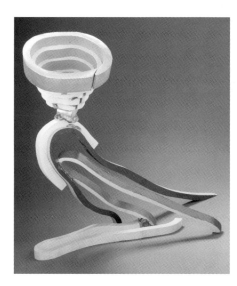

Untitled (Painted piece with orange Z at center), ca. 1985. Formed and welded aluminum, oil paint, automotive spray paint, 15½ x 19½ x 10½ in. Collection of John Adduci. Photo by Steve Greiner.

Untitled (Painted piece with long horizontal extension, bowl welded on), ca. 1985. Formed and welded aluminum, oil paint, automotive spray paint, 20½ x 18½ x 10 in. Collection of John Adduci. Photo by Steve Greiner.

Untitled (Painted piece leaning sharply to left, inverted dome at top left), ca. 1985. Formed and welded aluminum, oil paint, automotive spray paint, 24½ x 30 x 15 in. Collection of John Adduci. Photo by Steve Greiner.

to Honeybee, Kentucky, taking some of Steve's possessions with him, which he stored in a barn. These were lost when the barn burned down.[36]

In about 1990, Steve moved to Tempe, Arizona, where he lived with his retired parents and worked in their garage. During this time, Dan Blue and others in Chicago talked of an investment venture to bring Steve back to Chicago where he would make sculpture. Steve sent slides and documentation from Tempe. The painted constructions were photographed. These photos were shown to art dealers, but nothing happened.

The Final Years[37]

Larry Kornegay recalls Steve coming to Tempe in about 1990. In those days, Kornegay did studio production, sets and props for new product line introductions. Business was heavy in fall and winter, but much lighter in spring. Summer was the off-season. Kornegay employed artists in his business. He had been an artist himself, knew how they lived, and was cool with it. His artist employees worked overtime in the busy months, fattened their savings accounts, and drew on them to keep going while they made art.

Adduci, who knew Kornegay, told him that Steve might come to his office looking for work. When Steve turned up, he was living with his parents, making art in their garage, and he wanted a place of his own. Steve became a reliable employee who turned up every day for work and could do almost anything, says Kornegay. He'd work straight through until he was exhausted, rest for awhile, and then go back at it.

At one point, Steve had to put glitter on an object, something he'd never done before. He didn't know that glitter must be handled carefully or it gets everywhere. He lost control and Kornegay found him covered with the material, a comic sight.

At this time in his life, Steve preferred to stay in his apartment or studio. He had no girlfriends and did not go to nightclubs. He told Kornegay about the Sedgwick Studio sculptors and how much he enjoyed working with them. At Sedgwick, he could have beer whenever he wanted.

Throughout his time in Tempe, Steve kept busy in his studio. He made a series of small, colorful, abstract paintings that depicted cartoon-like people in different scenarios, and pedestal-sized polystyrene sculptures covered with Portland cement. These works have survived with his siblings in Berkeley and Tempe.

Lynn Urry visited Steve in Tempe and found him "working on a series of very interesting small sculptures that integrated abstract shapes with the real world." He made "an apartment building that portrayed burglars stealing a TV set escaping down the fire escape."

Babe Mobile, early 1990s. Foam, shaped with hot wire, dipped in liquid mixture containing Portland cement. Measurements unknown. Collection of Lynn Urry.

Lynn also remembers a "babe mobile . . . a convertible automobile with, in the back, a guy with a woman on either side and, in the front, the driver with a babe next to him on a drive in the country." These sculptures, Lynn explains, "were produced in foam that was shaped with a hot wire . . . The foam shapes were dipped in a mysterious mixture containing Portland cement."[58]

When Kornegay's work ran out, Steve moved back to his parents' garage, which had been converted into a studio and living area. He wanted to make art full time and to revive his career thereby. He sent photographs of his new work to the Phyllis Kind Gallery, not realizing that he had burned his bridges with her. After some months, the materials came back.

After that, says Janis, Steve "spent his days in the garage in a profound depression." His health failed. He thought that he had the flu, which left him with physical aches and a painful, lingering sore throat. His mother and sister tried to convince him to see a doctor, but he wouldn't listen. Unable to swallow food, he self-medicated, drinking eight cans of beer a day as his weight fell below 100 pounds.

When his mother pressed him to see a doctor, he left the house in his car and was discovered barely alive and taken to the hospital. The doctor told him that he had an inoperable case of esophageal cancer. The hospital attempted to treat him, but Steve went into a coma never to regain consciousness. On November 3, 1993, at the age of 54, Steve Urry died—much too soon.

[1] Robert Burns. "Giant Exhibition Has a Low Budget" *Grand Rapids Press* (September 2, 1973).

[2] Grand Rapids Art Museum, *Docent Training Part III, 1973* (Typewritten internal document supplied by GRAM).

[3] Grand Rapids Art Museum, Typewritten internal document with descriptions of exhibiting artists' work in *Sculpture Off the Pedestal, 1973, supplied by GRAM.*

[4] Keeler *op. cit.*

[5] Robert Burns. "Sculpture Eyed for City" *Muskegon Chronicle* (November 13, 1974).

[6] David Cooper. "New Sculpture—New Image: Grand Rapids' Grand Awakening," *Detroit Free Press* (November 18, 1973); Robert Burns. "Urry's 'Arch' Still a Question Mark for City" *The Muskegon Chronicle* (November 26, 1974); "Urry's 'Arch' on the Downtown Lakefront: Good Moves on the Waterfront by City—Chamber of Commerce" (Editorial) *The Muskegon Chronicle* (February 19, 1975); "Urry Arch Being Installed Today On Temporary Site at City Hall" *The Muskegon Chronicle* (ca. February 20, 1975); Joe Eyler. "They built Muskegon: Gone, but not Forgotten" *The Muskegon Chronicle* (January 31, 1980).

[7] Donald Miller. "Steel Art" *Pittsburgh Post-Gazette* (December 6, 1974), p. 25.

[8] "Alum Provides Material for Massive Art Work" *Carnegie Alumni News* (March 1975) p.1; "At Carnegie-Mellon: President Salutes Stainless Sculptor" *Pittsburgh Post-Gazette* (May 1975); Donald Miller. "Steven Urry's 30-Foot Work on CMU Campus: 'Reflections' Added to Outdoor Sculptures" *Pittsburgh Post-Gazette* (August 12, 1975); Conversation with David L. Beck, June 7, 2011.

[9] As of May 1, 1977, the piece was unharmed. A *Chicago Tribune* article described it as an "enormous geometric piece" that "has a permanent home on a grassy island in the center of a busy Pittsburgh thoroughfare." See Nessa Mines, "In Pittsburgh: Arts and crafts fest: Fun for everyone" *Chicago Tribune* (May 1, 1977).

[10] An undated, uncaptioned photograph among Steve Urry's papers shows two of the cut pieces on pedestals in an art gallery. The ad for Kent cigarettes appeared in *Art News*, vol. 73 (Summer 1974), Inner Back Cover. Beck did not meet Steve until 1975 and he has confirmed that most of the cut pieces were made in Chicago. They were probably shown at the Phyllis Kind Gallery where someone got the idea of using them in ads. Later, in New York, Steve made more cut pieces and showed them at the Zabriskie Gallery where they were photographed.

[11] This narrative is constructed from TG.1858.AM; an archive of the Nebraska I-80 Sculpture Project housed at the Nebraska State Historical Society, Lincoln. Steve submitted his project narrative on Playboy Bunny paper!

[12] "Geysers of Protest for Nebraska Art" *New York Times* (July 31, 1975), p. 32.

[13] Conversation with David L. Beck, January 16, 2012. It seems that Steve overcommitted and his resulting work schedule may have forced him to choose between completing the Nebraska commission by spring of 1976 and building the polyurethane isocyanate resin sculptures that he showed at the Hackley Museum and Grand Rapids Art Museum in late 1976 and early 1977. We have found no explanation for the long delays between the commissioning of the Nebraska sculpture and the promised beginning of work.

[14] Mary Baber photographed Steve in his Chicago studio during spring or summer of 1971. Vinyl hangings are visible in several photographs and in one (see page 19), Steve stands near a small inflated sculpture made of clear vinyl plastic.

[15] Michael Andre. *Art News*, vol. 72, (November 1973), p. 107.

[16] Jeremy Gilbert-Rolfe. *Artforum,* vol. 12, (December 1973), p. 89.

[17] *Contemporary American Painting and Sculpture,* Krannert Art Museum, Champaign, Illinois (March 10 - April 24, 1974).

[18] Zenith Insurance Company, *Isocyanates"* (Risk Management Bulletin) n.d. [Internet].

[19] According to Janis Urry, the machine that Steve used to make his polyurethane sculptures emitted noxious fumes and "was supposed to be used with shielding, which, of course, he ignored. This cavalier attitude, typical of Steve, foreshadowed things to come [i.e., the esophageal cancer that killed him]."

[20] Beck *op. cit.* Lynn Urry contributed to this description.

[21] Nancy Grove. "Steve Urry" *Arts,* vol. 50:5, p.5. The photograph is published above the review.

[22] http://muskegonartmuseum.org/component/content/article/8.

[23] Howarth to Urry July 28, 1975; Urry to Howarth September 9, 1975.

[24] "Urry Sculpture Exhibit" Hackley Art Museum press release (December 1976); Typewritten statement about Urry show (n.d., but probably written in December 1976) by Shirley Howarth; "Urry here to premiere work" *Muskegon Chronicle* (December 3, 1976).

[25] John Adduci supplied slides of the Muskegon show on which this account is based. Correspondence between Shirley Howarth and Steve Urry included a show inventory.

[26] Memorandum to John DeHorn from Mary Riordan, July 13, 1979 (parties unknown but probably associated with insurance firms).

[27] "A Summary of Damage and Repair" by Steven Urry, February 2 and February 9, 1977, (Muskegon Museum of Art files).

[28] M. David Distler of Bobrow Greenapple Burton Distler & Midler, New York, to David Bartlett of D&J Bartlett, Bronxville, New York, June 29, 1977. (Muskegon Museum of Art files.)

[29] Margaret Peterson, senior adjuster, Underwriters Adjusting Company, Grand Rapids, Michigan, to Fred Myers, director, Grand Rapids Art Museum, September 15, 1978, (Muskegon Museum of Art files). Sharon Hanks. "Damage to 'Indestructible' Sculptures Leads to Suit," *The Muskegon Chronicle* (January 10, 1980), p. 9 .

[30] Del Giorno *op.cit.*

[31] Beck *op.cit.*

[32] Adduci *op. cit*; Beck *op. cit.* Adduci says that when Steve was leaving the Wooster Street studio in 1981, he discarded his two-ingredient polyurethane equipment, cautioning the junkmen not to let the contents of the two drums mix. They ignored him and threw everything together in their truck, squashing the drums. The ingredients leaked, interacted, and the truck filled up with foam.

[33] This portion of the narrative is constructed from conversations and e-mails previously cited with Adduci, Scarff, and Peart. The author talked with Dan Blue, November 15, 2011.

[34] The Urry siblings all assert that Steve did not have a drinking problem, but he may have hidden it from them. They remember that he would have a drink at the end of the day, which is normal for many, but not that he drank to excess.

[35] Steve left five undated pages of hand-written notes in the Sedgwick Studios. These are now owned by Janis Urry. The writings place New York in Steve's past, which suggests a date after 1981. Here's a sample:

"In a period of time, I made shapes, put them every which way—am aware of them without conscious knowledge and they come together somehow."

"How to sustain, whatever this phenomenon is—is this what the I [Ching] teaches about innocence (no conscious motive)?"

[36] John Henry *op.cit.* John Henry trucked some of Steve's sculptures and other materials from Florida to Kentucky and stored them in a barn where a fire destroyed them. Henry owns one of Steve's sculptures and has loaned another to Chattanooga State Community College.

[37] Conversation with Larry Kornegay, July 18, 2011; Janis Urry *op. cit.*; the author visited the Urry home in 2011 and saw the work Steve did in Tempe.

[38] Among Steve's possessions in Tempe are Polaroid photographs of city scenes and the figure, in which he manipulated the emulsion to blur the image. Janis Urry believes that he took these photographs at some point in the mid-Seventies, possibly when he was married to Michelle.

Urry family ca. 1947 *(clockwise from top left):* Dion, Bill, Steve, Kay, Janis, Lynn.

Steve in San Francisco with 'Sun' painting ca. 1963.

Sprite, Jeb, Steve in Chicago late 1965.

Steve and Caleb in New York ca. 1977.

Caleb and Michelle Urry in New York ca. 1978.

CAREER HISTORY

Research for this section began with a two-page résumé that Steve Urry compiled. It documents his solo and group exhibitions: dates, locations, works shown, reviews, and show catalogs. Following are commissions that he completed, his presentations, journalistic accounts of his work and career, mentions in books, and his education. Not every citation is complete. When something listed in Urry's résumé could not be documented, it is listed at the end of the section.

SOLO EXHIBITIONS

1966 (November) Dell Gallery, Chicago, *Round Series*
Works Exhibited

Oop Zig. Welded steel, 80 x 30 x 20 in.

Round Two from *The Round Series.* Epoxy coated steel, 48 x 24 x 30 in.

Round Five from *The Round Series.* Epoxy coated steel, 102 x 48 x 6 in.

Round Six from *The Round Series.* Epoxy coated steel, 108 x 108 x 30 in.

Press

Barry, Edward. *Chicago Tribune,* November 20, 1966, p. F2.

Hayden, Harold. "Showcase," *Chicago Sun-Times,* November 20, 1966, p. 7.

Kind, Joshua. *Art News,* vol. 66, no.1, March 1967, p. 59.

1967, 1968 Midway Studios Exhibitions

After he returned from San Francisco in the summer of 1964, Urry had a working space in the Midway Studios at the University of Chicago, about a mile from his parents' home. In his résumé, Urry states that he had two solo exhibitions—*Round Series* in January of 1967, and a second untitled show in 1968—at the University of Chicago. These probably took place in the Midway Studios. Neither show is documented in university, art department records, in the *Maroon* (student newspaper), or in the Chicago press. See the narrative for more details.

1967 (October 14 - November 14) Royal Marks Gallery, New York, *Ribbon Farm*
Works Exhibited

Down Stream. Cast and welded aluminum, 104 x 90 x 102 in.

Head Flower. Cast and welded aluminum, 84 x 48 x 12 in.

Ribbon Check No. 1. Cast and welded aluminum, measurements unknown.

Round Five. Epoxy coated steel, 102 x 48 x 6 in.

Psychedilly Rose. Cast and welded aluminum, 126 x 176 x 98 in.

Waul Phaulderawl. Cast and welded aluminum, 90 x 50 x 27 in.

Press

Art in America, September 1967, vol. 55, p. 110

Art Scene magazine, Chicago, October 1967, vol. 1, no. 1, p. 27 (cartoon of a Urry sculpture).

Canaday, John. *New York Times,* October 21, 1967, p. 19.

Glueck, Grace. *New York Times,* October 29, 1967, p. 35.

Hayden, Harold. *Art News,* December 1967, vol. 66, p. 56.

Kozloff, Max. *Artforum,* December 1967, vol. 6, pp. 52-53.

Perrault, John. *Village Voice,* October 26, 1967.

R.N., *Arts,* December 1967 - January 1968, no. 42, p. 56.

Studio International, September 1967, no. 174, p. 123 (one-paragraph notice includes photo of *Round 5*).

1968 Headscape Exhibition

In 1968, Urry exhibited his aluminum sculpture *Headscape* (cast and welded aluminum: 13 x 25 x 30 ft.) on the campuses of De Paul University, the University of Chicago, Northern Illinois University, Barat College, and Loyola University. That same year, it was shown in downtown Chicago in *Eight American Sculptors,* a group exhibition. *Headscape* was destroyed in 1970. For details, see narrative.

Press

"News Briefs," *Chicago Tribune,* February 26, 1968, p. 3 (short article indicates that *Headscape* was brought to the University of Chicago campus for exhibition in six pieces and assembled).

1969 (July 19 – September 7) Museum of Contemporary Art, Chicago, *Dribblescapes*
Works Exhibited

Large Cloud. Welded cast and hammered aluminum, 35 x 15 ft.

Cloud Flower (also known as *Small Cloud).* Welded cast and hammered aluminum, 15 x 10 x 5 ft.

Dribble Dot. Welded cast and hammered aluminum, multipart sculpture covered a 48 in. square area.

Polka-Dotted Earth Mother. Welded cast and hammered aluminum, 16 x 4.6 x 8 ft.

Moon Ribbon (original title was *Ribbon Flowering Dotscape).* Welded cast and hammered aluminum, 308 x 96 x 120 in.

Press

Anderson, Don J. *Chicago Today*, July 27, 1969, p. 15.

Hayden, Harold. *Chicago Sun-Times*, June 15, 1969, p. 14.

Hayden, Harold. *Chicago Sun-Times*, August 17, 1969, p. 9.

Mark, Norman. *Chicago Daily News*, July 26, 1969, p. 9 (interview article includes photograph of *Dribblescapes*).

Schulze, Franz. *Chicago Daily News*, July 26, 1969, p. 9.

Willis, Thomas. *Key*, August 2, 1969, pp. 18-25.

Willis, Thomas. *Where* magazine, August 9, 1969, p. 15.

1969 (October 21 – November 15) Zabriskie Gallery, New York

On October 29, 1969, Urry consigned the following cast and welded aluminum sculptures to Zabriskie Gallery:

Vacuole, 14.5 x 13.5 in.

Dribbledown, 11.25x 14.75 in.

Moratorium, 40.5 x 36 in.

Moonbeams, 27.5x 38 in.

Small Cloud Flower, 180 x 120 x 60 in.

Large Winged Thing, 75 x 51 in.

Earth Mother, 192 x 56 x 96 in.

He also consigned 11 pencil drawings.

Works Exhibited

Moon Ribbon, cast and welded aluminum, 308 x 96 x 120 in.

Earth Mother, cast and welded aluminum, 16 x 4.6 x 8 ft.

Large Cloud, cast and welded aluminum, 35 x 15 ft.

Untitled, cast and welded aluminum, 120 x 96 x 96 in.

Small Cloud, cast and welded aluminum, 15 x 10 x 5 ft.

Press

Art News, December 1969, vol. 68, p. 71.

Pincus-Witten, Robert. *Artforum*, January 1970, p. 65.

Arts Magazine, no. 44, December 1969 - January 1970, p. 57.

1971 (Opened November 19) Phyllis Kind Gallery, Chicago

Works Exhibited

The author has not found any record of what was shown, but, on June 11, 1971, the Phyllis Kind Gallery acknowledged the following works taken on consignment and presumably priced by Urry:

Mini Blatt (measurements unknown). $1,250.

Shimi Blatt (measurements unknown). $600.

Polka Dots and Moon Beams (measurements unknown). $1,500.

Ribbon Arrow (measurements unknown). $1,000.

Quiver (measurements unknown). $1,150.

Large Winged Thing, 75 x 51 in. $2,500.

Footed Ribbon Flower, cast and welded aluminum, 19 x 7 x 24 in. $1,100.

Wanderlust, cast and welded aluminum, 47 x 20 x 32 in. $2,000.

Press

Allen, Jane, and Guthrie, Derek. "Gallery Notes," *Chicago Tribune*, May 14, 1971, p. Q18 (Urry listed as a Phyllis Kind artist).

Allen, Jane, and Guthrie, Derek. "A Grab Bag of Art Ready for Plucking," *Chicago Tribune,* September 26, 1971, p. E8 (announcement of the forthcoming show).

Allen, Jane, and Guthrie, Derek. "Second City Sculpture," *Chicago Tribune,* December 12, 1971, p. K22 (reviews Phyllis Kind Gallery exhibit).

1972 (February 8 – March 4) Zabriskie Gallery, New York

In 1971, Urry priced and consigned the following pieces to the Zabriskie Gallery:

Wanderlust, cast and welded aluminum, 47 x 20 x 32 in. $2,000.

Footed Ribbon Flower, cast and welded aluminum, 19 x 7 x 24 in. $1,100.

Untitled, cast and welded aluminum, 42 x 16 x 34 in. $2,400.

In his letter of transmittal, Urry stated that "Above pieces all in highly polished aluminum . . . I believe they were all done in 1970."

Works Exhibited

Framescape, cast and welded aluminum, 54 x 45 x 30 in.

Horizontal Ribbon Scape, cast and welded aluminum, 39 x 79 x 42 in.

Loop & Spiral Scape, cast and welded aluminum, 46 x 54 x 30 in.

Affirmation, cast and welded aluminum, 53 x 28 x 38 in.
Underflow, cast and welded aluminum, 25 x 48 x 22 in.
Horizontal Spiral, cast and welded aluminum, 8 x 10 x 17 in.
Inside Sound, cast and welded aluminum, 17 x 13 x 15 in.
Art Deco Piece, cast and welded aluminum, 10 x 10 x 7 in.
Vertical Spiral, cast and welded aluminum, 9 x 9 x 10 in.
Loop, cast and welded aluminum, 12 x 10 x 7 in.

Press

Art News, vol. 70, February 1972, p. 206.

Arts, no. 46, March 1972, p. 69.

Shirey, David L. *New York Times*, February 26, 1972.

1973 (September 11-29) Zabriskie Gallery, New York

Works Exhibited

Sculpture for One Room, 1973, inflatable vinyl, 144 x 420 x 120 in.

Press

Andre, Michael. *Art News,* vol. 72, p. 107, November 1973; Gilbert-Rolfe, Jeremy. *Artforum,* vol. 12, p. 89, December 1973.

1976 (January) Zabriskie Gallery, New York

Works Exhibited

Expanded large-scale polyurethane isocyanate sculptures (See text for details).

Press

Grove, Nancy. *Arts,* no. 50, p.5, January 1976 (includes color photograph).

1976-77 (December 3, 1976 - January 2, 1977) Hackley Art Museum (now the Muskegon Museum of Art, Muskegon, Michigan)

Works Exhibited

Untitled #1, polyurethane isocyanate resin, 132 x 84 x 84 in.
Untitled #2, polyurethane isocyanate resin, 84 x 144 x 96 in.
Untitled #3, polyurethane isocyanate resin, 120 x 240 x 96 in.
Untitled #4, polyurethane isocyanate resin, 60 x 60 x 60 in.
Untitled #5, polyurethane isocyanate resin, 72 x 60 x 60 in.
Untitled #6, polyurethane isocyanate resin, 48 x 48 x 48 in.

Four smaller aluminum works

17 pencil sketches

It is not clear from Hackley Museum records whether five or six of the polyurethane isocyanate resin sculptures were shown. Urry may have brought six pieces and shown only five.

1977 (January 7 - February 1) Grand Rapids Art Museum, Michigan

Works Exhibited (*Same works as above.*)

NOTE: This show was organized by the Hackley Art Museum. Urry brought the sculptures from New York in a truck. After the Hackley show came down, Urry was flown to Muskegon where he and a Grand Rapids Art Museum employee packed the work and trucked it to the Grand Rapids Art Museum. When the Grand Rapids show came down, Urry was not present and the sculptures were incorrectly packed before being trucked to New York. They were completely destroyed upon arrival and a lawsuit followed (See narrative for details).

Press

Hanks, Sharon. "Suit Claims Museum Responsible For Destruction of Five Sculptures" *Grand Rapids Press,* January 1980.

Hanks, Sharon. "Damage to 'indestructible' sculptures leads to suit" *The Muskegon Chronicle,* January 10, 1980, p. 9.

GROUP EXHIBITIONS

1962 (June 4 - June 15), *Spring Show,* San Francisco Art Institute, San Francisco.
Exhibited two metal sculptures in this show of more than 200 student works selected by faculty. Urry is not mentioned in any press releases, but publicity materials were sent to Chicago newspapers and a brief notice appeared in the *Chicago Daily News.*

1965 (November 14 - December 17), *Phalanx 3,* Illinois Institute of Technology, Chicago.
Urry was one of 85 artists in this show (each represented by two works), which was organized by Participating Artists of Chicago, a committee of local artists. A press release states: "Organized by the artists themselves, the exhibition is intended to provide a more ample coverage of current developments than can be obtained through the Art Institute Annual and the offerings of the galleries. PHALANX 3 has the further intention of bringing young, promising talent to the attention of the discerning public, and to arouse recognition of the scope and variety inherent in the art of Chicago." A show catalog was promised, but none has been found.

Press: Kind, Joshua. "ArtNews from Chicago," *Art News,* vol. 64, no. 10, February 1966, p. 46; "New Exhibit in HUB, Phalanx 3, Opens Sunday," *Technology News (Illinois Institute of Technology),* vol. 79, no. 9, November 12, 1965; Schulze, Franz. "Some Final Thoughts About Phalanx 3," *Daily News Panorama,* December 18, 1965, p. 17.

1966 (May), *New Horizons in Sculpture,* Marina City, Chicago. Showed *Spring Bubble* (dimensions unknown).
Press: Barry, Edward. "Art Note," *Chicago Tribune,* May 11, 1966, p. B4 (says that Urry won the $750 first prize in this show).
Barry, Edward. "The North Shore's League of Super Patrons," *Chicago Tribune,* September 8, 1968, p. J 42 (says that this show helped Urry "to national prominence.")

1966 (July 5 - 22), Kendall College, Evanston, Illinois. According to a Kendall College press release, the college, "in cooperation with Phalanx, the Chicago artists' association," presented "a large exhibition (called *The Heavy Show*) of Chicago sculpture in its auditorium-in-the-round." Urry participated in this exhibition, but the work he showed is unknown.

1967 (Feburary), *Urry/Holbrook in New York.* According to the painter Steven Holbrook, Marjorie Dell, the Chicago art dealer who represented Urry and Holbrook, found the two artists a temporary loft space near Bryant Park in New York City. They drove out, installed their work in the loft, and approached art dealers in person. This private show was intended to get their work out in New York. There was no press. For details see narrative.

1967 (March 3 - April 2), *70th Annual Exhibition of Artists of Chicago and Vicinity,* Art Institute of Chicago.
Shown: *Blat* Steel, 83 x 78 x 42 in. (1966-67). Awarded the Emilie L. Wilde Prize of $500 and the Union Carbide Corporation, Linde Division Award of $200.
Press: Barry, Edward. "70th Chicago Art Show Opens," *Chicago Tribune,* March 3, 1967, p. B17 (describes *Blat* as "a tremendous construction of welded steel"); "That Art Institute Show Draws Mail," *Chicago Tribune,* March 26, 1967, p. E2; *Hyde Park Herald,* vol. 86, April 6, 1967, p. 4.
Catalog: Art Institute of Chicago, *70th Annual Exhibition by Artists of Chicago and Vicinity* Chicago, Art Institute of Chicago, 1967. (*Blat* was published as #71 in this catalog.)

1967 (November 3-30), *The GAS CITY Point of View,* Welna Gallery, Chicago. Exhibiting were Urry, Michael Hall, John Henry, David Middlebrook, Robert Ray, and Tom Steger. According to Michael Hall, this show was "something of a farce." Welna Gallery was "basically a vanity gallery and John Henry found out that it was going to be vacant for a few weeks in November 1967. He subsequently 'booked' us into the space for that time slot. I saw the show and was underwhelmed. It came and went with no reviews and no sales. The poster was the thing."

1968, *Fourth Annual Fine Arts Festival of Northern Illinois University,* Fine Arts Building, NIU, De Kalb, Illinois.
Shown: *Headscape* (see *Exhibitions of Headscape* above, also narrative).
Press: "Art Notes," *Chicago Tribune,* February 11, 1968, p. F2.

1968, *Illinois Sculptors '68-'70,* a traveling exhibition organized by the Illinois Arts Council, an agency of the State of Illinois, in cooperation with the Illinois Sesquicentennial Commission and the Illinois State Museum. This exhibition of 23 sculptors was curated by Richard Hunt. Urry showed *Loyola Commission Model* (welded aluminum, 35 x 6 in.) and *Flower Power* (welded aluminum, 60 x 36 in.).
Press: Stone, Dennis. "Chicago At Mid-Season," *Art Scene,* vol. 2, no. 3 and 4, December 1968/January 1969, pp. 36-39. Stone cites Urry's participation in *Eight American Sculptors* and publishes a photograph of *Flower Power.* In commenting on the *Whitney Annual* exhibition, Stone writes that "if dedication and hard work had been the major criteria for selection, Steve Urry and John Henry would have been included (with other Chicago sculptors) in this exhibition."; Hough, Mary Pat. "Art: Sculpture Goes on Tour," *Chicago Tribune,* December 1, 1968, p. A 6.
Catalog: *Illinois Sculptors '68-'70,* Chicago, Huron Press, 1968. Unpaged four-volume catalog. *Loyola Commission Model* is published in volume four.

1968 (April 6 - October 6), *American Pavilion at Hemisfair,* San Antonio, Texas.
Shown: *Psychedilly Rose.*

1968 (May 5 - June 2), *Exhibition 150.* Barat College, Lake Forest, Illinois. Urry exhibited *Headscape* in this exhibition of 30 paintings and sculptures by 11 Chicago artists that honored the Illinois sesquicentennial. Barat published a 28-page catalog of the exhibition entitled *Exhibition 150,* which included a brief résumé and a portrait photograph.
Press: "Art Notes" *Chicago Tribune,* May 5, 1968, p. F2; "Art Exhibit Opens at Barat" *Chicago Tribune,* May 5, 1968, p. N5; "11 Artists to Exhibit 30 Works at Barat," *Chicago Tribune,* May 16, 1968, p. N11; Carole Edwards, "Rosary College to Display Student Art," *Chicago Tribune,* May 2, 1968, p. S10.

1968 (May 5 - June 5), *18th Annual University of Chicago Festival of the Arts presents Three Sculptors: John Henry, Robert Ray, Steve Urry.* Showed *Headscape* (see Exhibitions of Headscape above, also narrative).

1968 (October 6 - November 4), *Eight American Sculptors,* Pioneer Court Plaza, Chicago.
Shown: *Headscape* (see Exhibitions of *Headscape* above). John Henry organized this show of contemporary sculpture in downtown Chicago, which helped pave the way for public acceptance of large outdoor work by living artists. See narrative for details.

1969 (April 22 - June 1), *Society for Contemporary Art Exhibition,* Art Institute of Chicago. The Society for Contemporary Art is a support group of the Art Institute of Chicago. It sponsors lectures and purchases work by living artists which it presents to the museum. Showed *Untitled* (1969).
Press: Barry, Edward. "Well Ahead of the Avant-Garde" *Chicago Tribune,* May 18, 1969, p. G2.
Catalog: *Society for Contemporary Art 29th Annual Exhibition,* Chicago: Art Institute of Chicago, 1969. Four-page unillustrated pamphlet lists Urry's *Untitled.*

1970 (September 11 - November 15), *American Sculpture: An Exhibition Organized to Inaugurate the Sheldon Sculpture Garden at the University of Nebraska, Lincoln.* This exhibition was organized by Sheldon Museum director Norman A. Geske and intended as a complete survey of the history of American sculpture. Showed *Psychedilly Rose.* See narrative for details.
Catalog: *American Sculpture: An Exhibition Organized to Inaugurate the Sheldon Sculpture Garden at the University of Nebraska, Lincoln.* Lincoln, Nebraska Art Association, 1970. *Psychedilly Rose* is published as sculpture #165.

1971 (March 13 - April 18), *73rd Annual Exhibition of Artists of Chicago and Vicinity,* Art Institute of Chicago.
Shown: *Ribbon Loop* (n.d.). Presumably cast and welded aluminum, measurements unknown.
Press: Wells, Daniel. "Galleries: Chicago Artists Make, Show Work," *Chicago Tribune,* March 28, 1971, p. E7 (calls *Ribbon Loop* "the best sculpture in the show").
Catalog: *73rd Annual Exhibition of Artists of Chicago and Vicinity,* Art Institute of Chicago, 1971. *Ribbon Loop* is published as catalog number 70.

1972 (May 13 - June 25), *Chicago Imagist Art,* Museum of Contemporary Art, Chicago.
Shown: *Check the Pyramids Xing,* 1965, welded steel, 84 x 64 x 82 in.; *Downstream,* 1966, cast and welded aluminum, 104 x 104 x 80 in.; and *Popeil Commission,* 1971, cast and welded aluminum, 60 x 24 x 18 in.
Press: "Gallery Notes," *Chicago Tribune,* May 7, 1972, p. Q18; "Far-out Fantasies from Chicago Artists," *Chicago Tribune,* May 14, 1972, p. Q1.
Catalog: *Chicago Imagist Art.* Chicago: Museum of Contemporary Art, 1972. The unpaged catalog lists Urry's works in the show and publishes *Downstream,* 1965. For details, see narrative.

1972 (March 18 - 20), *Winter Show 1972,* West Suburban Temple Har Zion Sisterhood, River Forest, Illinois.
Shown: *Moon Ribbon,* cast and welded aluminum, 308 x 96 x 120 in., and *Cloud Flower* (also known as *Small Cloud),* welded cast and hammered aluminum, 180 x 120 x 60 in.
Press: "The Man and the Moon," *Chicago Tribune,* Mar. 5, 1972, p. W10. Photo shows Urry with *Moon Ribbon and Cloud Flower.*

1972 (Early September to September 29), *One Illinois Center,* One Illinois Center, Chicago.
Shown: *Downstream,* 1966, cast and welded aluminum, 104 x 104 x 80 in.
Press: "Art Happening on Wacker Drive," *Chicago Tribune,* May 28, 1972, p. C1 (announces that Urry will show his work in fall); Adrian, Dennis. "Let's show off more sculpture downtown like Steve Urry's," *Chicago Daily News Panorama,* September 9-10, 1972, p. 6; Allen, Jane and Guthrie, Derek. "New City Plazas Provide Vistas for Forgotten Sculptures," *Chicago Tribune,* September 10, 1972, p. M22, (review includes photo of *Downstream*).

1973 (March 30 - May 6), *Art Institute of Chicago 74th Annual Exhibition of Artists of Chicago and Vicinity,* Chicago.
Shown: *Bronze Arch No. 1,* 1972, bronze, 24 x 8 x 4 in.
Press: Allen, Jane and Guthrie, Derek. "Travelers on the Only Avenue to the Place of Pride," *Chicago Tribune,* April 1, 1973, p. F25.
Catalog: *74th Annual Exhibition of Artists of Chicago and Vicinity.* Art Institute of Chicago, 1973. *Bronze Arch No. 1* is No. 124.

1973 (September 8 - December 3), *Sculpture Off the Pedestal,* Grand Rapids Museum of Art, Michigan.
Shown: *Arch,* 1973, welded aluminum painted white, 252 x 72 x 48 in.
Press: Makanson, Joy. *The Sunday News,* Detroit, September 16, 1973, p. 4-E, (photograph of *Arch* stating that it was exhibited in Grand Rapids); *The Grand Rapids Press,* August 12, 1973, (announces the show), and September 8, 1973 (photograph of *Arch);* O'Doherty, Brian. *Art in America,* vol. 62, January 1974, pp. 78-79 (photograph of *Arch*).
Catalog: *Sculpture Off the Pedestal,* Grand Rapids Art Museum, Michigan, 1973. Publishes *Arch,* a résumé, and a photograph of Urry.

1974 (March 10 - April 21), *Contemporary American Painting and Sculpture,* Krannert Art Museum, University of Illinois, Urbana-Champaign.
Shown: *Untitled,* 1973, inflatable vinyl, 144 x 420 x 120 in.
Catalog: *Contemporary American Painting and Sculpture,* Urbana: University of Illinois Press, 1974. Publishes *Untitled* on p. 124.

1974 (May), *The Chicago Style,* four-part exhibition curated by Dennis Adrian at Center for Continuing Education, University of Chicago.
Shown: *Untitled,* ca.1965, in the fourth part of this show.
Press: Forwalter, John. "Into the Work," *Hyde Park Herald,* vol. 92, p. 24, May 15, 1974.

1976 (July - August), *American Salon des Refusés,* Stamford Museum and Nature Center, Connecticut. *Outlook,* July 1976, a Stamford Museum member publication, calls this exhibition "basically an extension of the bicentennial sculpture show now at the Whitney Museum in New York City and includes those artists whose works could not be shown in the Whitney." The August *Outlook* states that a Urry sculpture was chosen for its indoor show, but provides no name or description.

1977 (May), *57th Street Art Fair,* Chicago.
Press: *Hyde Park Herald,* vol. 95, no. 2, May 4 and vol. 95, no. 20, May 11.

1978 (March 17 - April 23), *CHICAGO: The City and Its Artists 1945-1978,* The University of Michigan Museum of Art, Ann Arbor.
Shown: *Oop-Zig,* iron, 80 x 30 x 20 in.
Catalog: *Chicago: The City and its Artists 1945-1978,* the University of Michigan Art Gallery, Ann Arbor, 1978. The essays "Sculpture in Chicago" calls Urry and John Henry "direct metal sculptors." The catalog publishes *Oop-Zig,* a résumé, and one of the untitled foam sculptures from the 1977

Hackley Museum show; *Arch*; and *Reflections,* stainless steel, 180 x 540 x 420 in., which was commissioned by Carnegie-Mellon University, Pittsburgh.

1981 (February 12 - March 28), *Recent Trends in Collecting: Twentieth Century Painting and Sculpture from the National Museum of American Art,* National Museum of American Art, Washington, D.C.
Shown: *Untitled,* 1970, cast and welded aluminum 34 x 40.75 x 22.25 in.
Catalog: McAllister, Jane, ed. *Recent Trends in Collecting: Twentieth Century Painting and Sculpture from the National Museum of American Art,* Washington, D.C. Published for the National Museum of American Art by the Smithsonian Institution Press, 1982. Publishes *Untitled* on p. 62 with accompanying text.

1989 (May 12-16), *Metal Works,* Chicago. According to Jerry Peart, this was probably an exhibition in the Sedgwick Studio where Steve Urry worked with John Adduci, Tom Scarff, Jerry Peart, and others. The show would have been up during Art Expo 1989. According to John Adduci, Metalworks Gallery was a short-lived Chicago space where local sculptors had a group show. Adduci's rock and roll band, *The Art Throbs,* played there at the opening in a battle of the bands, he says. *The Art Throbs* lost the battle, but won the war "by having the tools to open the keg."

1995 (April 26 - June 1), *Post War Chicago: Works on Paper and Sculpture* , Smart Gallery, University of Chicago. The museum presumably showed *Untitled*, 1971, cast and welded aluminum, 9.25 x 10.5 in. and/or *Arch,* 1972, cast bronze, 15 x 5 x 5 in. from its collection.
Press: Glatt, Cara. "Exhibit shows Chicago artists post-war outlook,"*Hyde Park Herald,* April 26, 1995, p. 8.

1996 (November 16, 1996 - March 23, 1997), *Art in Chicago 1945-1995,* Museum of Contemporary Art, Chicago. This exhibition, which was the first comprehensive show of postwar Chicago art history, opened three years after Urry's death.
Shown: *Blat,* 1966-67, steel, 83 x 78 x 42 in.
Press: Artner, Alan. "Museum of Contemporary Art A History That Defeats Itself in its Survey of 50 Years of Chicago Art, the MCA Wrongly Puts Order Ahead of Glorious Chaos," *Chicago Tribune,* November 24, 1996, p. 1; Buchholz, Barbara B. "Chicago's Style Gutsy, Independent, Defiant: A New Show Captures Our Artistic Traits,"*Chicago Tribune,* December 1, 1996, p. 15; Vine, Richard. "Where the Wild Things Were,"*Art in America,* vol. 85, no. 5, May 1997, pp. 98-111(calls *Blat* a "jagged seven-foot-high loop of cut steel").
Catalog: *Art in Chicago, 1945-1995,* New York, Thames and Hudson, 1996, publishes *Blat,* p.180, commentary, p. 78, and a biography, p. 287.

2001, *International Sculpture Center Connection IV,* Wood Street Gallery, Chicago.
Shown: *Psychedilly Rose II,* cast and welded aluminum, 105 x 68 x 24 in. Urry's sculpture was donated to this show which benefitted the International Sculpture Center. The sculpture is now at the Museum of Outdoor Arts, Englewood, Colorado.

2011 (January 29 - May 29), *Seeing is a Kind of Thinking: A Jim Nutt Companion,* Museum of Contemporary Art, Chicago.
Shown: *Double X,* lacquered steel, 83.5 x 77 x 42.25 in., as part of this group exhibition of work by artists who worked in Chicago at the same time as the painter Jim Nutt.

UNDOCUMENTED GROUP EXHIBITIONS

1966 (summer), *Purdue University;* **1966** (April), *Exhibition Chicago,* University of Illinois Circle Campus; **1970,** *WMAA;* **1980,** Michigan, *Public Sculpture Artrain Traveling Exhibition.*

COMMISSIONS

1968 Loyola University, Chicago
As described in Reidy's *Chicago Sculpture,* Loyola University commissioned a sculpture for the façade of the Elizabeth M. Cudahy Memorial Library on its Chicago Lake Shore campus. For details see narrative.

1970 Floyd Abramson, Chicago
Included were a suspended piece and a four-foot pedestal piece, which were placed in Abramson's Chicago home.

1971 Popeil Brothers, Inc., Chicago
Urry made a tall arch-like piece in cast and welded aluminum and an aluminum chess set. The arch-like piece is untraced. Some chess pieces remain in family hands.

1975 Carnegie-Mellon University, Pittsburgh
Called *Reflections,* this stainless steel sculpture was made when Urry was teaching for half a semester at Carnegie-Mellon University. For details see narrative.

1976 Nebraska Bicentennial Interstate 80 Sculpture
According to the Web site of the Sheldon Museum (www.sheldonartmuseum.org/education/I-80/works.html), "Two artists were unable to complete and install their work because of a major delay in the fundraising process necessitated by the legislature's decision to hold public hearings regarding acceptance of the sculptures." Urry's projected 22 x 10 x 25 ft. aluminum sculpture *Platte River Ribbon* was to be sited at the Cozad rest stop on I-80 next to the Platte River. For details see narrative.

Untraced Commissions: 1975, Shire National Corp, Parsippany, New Jersey; 1976, R. Lavin & Sons, North Chicago, Illinois (Commission was a bronze wall piece.)

PRESENTATIONS

1968 School of the Art Institute of Chicago
Urry was an instructor in the Sculpture Studio during summer of 1968. According to James Zanzi of the School of the Art Institute of Chicago, this class was a grand success and he wanted Urry back in fall, but it did not happen. For details see narrative.

1970 Cranbrook Academy, Bloomfield Hills, Michigan
According to Michael Hall who was head of sculpture (artist in residence) at Cranbrook from 1970 to 1990, he invited Urry to be a visiting artist in the sculpture department for "a three- or four-day stint." For details see narrative.

1974-1975 Carnegie-Mellon University, Pittsburgh
Urry was hired to teach for a half semester in 1974-1975, but stayed considerably longer, building a stainless steel sculpture *Reflections* on the campus and later in an off-campus studio (see **Commissions** p. 67). For details see narrative.

UNDOCUMENTED PRESENTATIONS

Ca. 1969 University of California, Berkeley
Lecturer, summer quarter. Letters exist between Urry and UC Berkeley, but it is not clear that this happened.

1971, 1972 University of Kentucky, Lexington
Michael Hall, the sculptor, taught at the University of Kentucky from 1966 to 1970. Hall thinks that the faculty members who succeeded him may have invited Urry to be an artist in residence at brief workshops.

NEWS AND FEATURE ARTICLES

1966
Robertson, Nan. "Arts Council Focuses on Filmmakers," *New York Times,* December 20, 1966, p. 39.
"National Arts Council Announces Awards," *Chicago Tribune,* December 20, 1966, p. B1. (Urry receives a $5,000 award from the National Council on the Arts.)

1968
Boyer, Brian D. "Up from Chicago: How a Nice Young Sculptor Crashed New York," *Chicago Tribune,* April 21, 1968, p. H36. (Amusing account of Urry's first New York show at Royal Marks Gallery—making the work in Chicago, truck trip to New York, and adventures there. A brief teaser extract from this article appears in the *Chicago Tribune,* April 21, 1968, p. F4.)

1969
"Aluminum Flame," *Chicago Tribune,* March 23, 1969, p. W15. (Photo shows high school students looking at a Urry sculpture.)
Nelson, Susan. "Walking Tour: Continuing North in Lincoln Avenue," *Chicago Tribune,* August 15, 1969, p. B11. (Article mentions Urry studio above the Biograph Theater.)
Boyer, Brian D., photos by Larry Graf, "Steven Jay Urry Isn't Practical About Anything," *Chicago Sun-Times Midwest Magazine,* September 14, 1969, pp. 35-36. (Entertaining if inaccurate account of Urry's life and work in the Lincoln Avenue studio.)

1971
Page, Eleanor. "Paging People: Radcliffe's Art Tour," *Chicago Tribune,* March 29, 1971, p. B10. (Group to visit Urry studio.)
Moore, Patricia. "Artists Live, Work Big," *Chicago Daily News,* April 30, 1971, p. 21.
Anderson, Donald James. "Urry *Dribblescapes* bump and burp sculpture," *Chicago Magazine,* May/June 1971, pp. 7-9.
Schulze, Franz. "Art News in Chicago," *Art News,* vol. 70, November 1971, pp. 48-55, 59.

1974
Sculpture Off the Pedestal, a group exhibition in 1973, led to the sale of *Arch* to the City of Muskegon, Michigan. Articles in local newspapers about *Arch* include:
"Sculpture Eyed for City," *Muskegon Chronicle,* November 13, 1974.
Burns, Robert. "Urry's Arch Still a Question Mark for City," *Muskegon Chronicle,* November 26, 1974.
"City's Sculptured Arch is Going to Muskegon," *Grand Rapids Press,* November 28, 1974.
"Arch, 1973, Great Symbol of Future Progress" (letter to the editor), *Muskegon Chronicle,* 1974.
Miller, Donald. "Steel Art," *Pittsburgh Post-Gazette,* December 6, 1974. (Urry teaching at Carnegie-Mellon and construction of his sculpture *Reflections*)
ArtNews, vol. 73, Summer 1974. Advertisement for Kent cigarettes featuring Urry's work on inner back cover.

1975

"Lakefront Site Picked for Muskegon's Arch," *Muskegon Chronicle,* February 12, 1975.

"Good Moves on the Waterfront by City—Chamber of Commerce," *Muskegon Chronicle,* February 19, 1975, p. 4.

"Urry Arch Being Installed Today On Temporary Site at City Hall," *Muskegon Chronicle,* February 1975.

"Urry Has Its Big Day," *Muskegon Chronicle,* 1975.

Helfrich, Hal. "Alum Provides Material for Massive Art Work," *Carnegie Alumni News* (published for the Alumni of Carnegie-Mellon University, Pittsburgh), March 1975, pp. 1-2 (describes how Urry transformed a gift of stainless steel sheets from David M. Schmid, a Carnegie-Mellon alumnus).

Luecking, Stephen. "Off the Pedestal: Chicago + Public Sculpture 1965 to 1975," *Sculpture,* May/June, 1975, vol. 17, no. 5, pp. 40-45. (This history of public sculpture activity in Chicago mentions Urry.)

"At Carnegie-Mellon: President Salutes Stainless Sculptor" *Pittsburgh Post-Gazette,* May 1975 (photograph with long caption that describes *Reflections,* Urry's stainless steel, 96 x 360 in., Sculpture installed on the Carnegie-Mellon University campus).

"Geysers of Protest for Nebraska Art" *New York Times,* July 31, 1975, p. 32. Urry is a sculptor on this project. (See **Commissions,** p. 67), also narrative.

Miller, Donald. "Steve Urry's 30-Foot Work on CMU Campus: 'Reflections' Added to Outdoor Sculptures" *Pittsburgh Post-Gazette,* August 12, 1975, p. 6 (announces completion of *Reflections*).

1976

"10 Win Contest on Road Sculpture," *New York Times,* July 10, 1976. (Urry has won a commission for the Nebraska Bicentennial Interstate 80 Sculpture Garden.)

Schjeldahl, Peter. "Letter from Chicago," *Art in America,* July/August 1976, vol. 64, no. 4, pp. 52-58. (Urry mentioned in a survey of Chicago art.)

Kuspit, Donald. "Regionalism Reconsidered," *Art in America,* July/August 1976, vol. 64, no. 4, pp. 64-69.

Dean, Andrea O. "Grand Rapids Becomes a Showplace of the Use of Sculpture in Public Places," *American Institute of Architects Journal,* October 1976, pp. 42-43.

Allen, Jane and Guthrie, Derek. "Interview with Three Chicago Sculptors," *New Art Examiner,* vol. 4, no. 2, November 1976, pp. 4-5. (John Henry, Jerry Peart, and Barry Tinsley are interviewed. Henry describes conditions for sculptors in Chicago, says that he and Urry were once the only two large-scale sculptors in Chicago.)

1977

"Urry Here to Premiere Work," *Muskegon Chronicle,* 1977. (Urry is in Muskegon to assemble *Arch* for showing before it goes on national tour.)

Mines, Nessa. "In Pittsburgh: Arts and Crafts Fest: Fun for Everyone," *Chicago Tribune,* May 1, 1977, p. C10. (*Reflections* has "a permanent home on a grassy island in the center of a busy Pittsburgh thoroughfare.")

1979

"Chicago Art Off to DC," *Chicago Sun-Times Show,* May 20, 1979, p. 4. (Samuel Koffler has given his collection of Chicago art, including work by Urry, to the National Gallery, Washington, D.C.)

1998

Luecking, Stephen. *Jerry Peart,* catalog of one-man show at Gahlberg Gallery, College of DuPage, Glen Ellyn, Illinois. ("*Steppin' Out,*" the catalog introduction calls Urry an influence on Peart.)

2005

Art Walk at Oakton, Oakton Community College, Des Plaines, Illinois. Catalog describes Oakton's outdoor art collection. (Jerry Peart, one of the artists in the collection, says that he came to Chicago from Arizona when Urry asked him to help out on a project.)

2008

The Museum of Outdoor Arts Collection, Museum of Outdoor Arts, 2008, Englewood, Colorado. Photograph of *Psychedilly Rose II,* p. 8.

(Text reads: "One of a small number of artists who shaped public sculpture in the U.S. in the 1960s and 1970s, Steve Urry defied the paradigm that previously governed metal sculpture in the early 20th century. He went against the industrial style of the Cubists and Constructivists. Instead, Urry refined his craft through his unique approach to space and form. Urry's composition leads the viewer through a trail of fluid, organic lines in space. The artist 'exploits an enormous strength-to-weight ratio while contorting and enlivening the space.'")

BOOKS (in chronological order)

Meilach, Dona Z. and Seiden, Don. *Direct Metal Sculpture: Creative Techniques and Appreciation,* New York, Crown Publishers, 1966. Pages 100-102 describe Urry's fabrication technique. "In this series," says the text, "Steve Urry demonstrates the methods he uses to build up a sculpture which states an exciting, personal, intelligent relationship between organic and geometric forms. Urry uses an oxyacetylene torch for cutting and an arc-welding unit for fusing the sheet metal." *Check the Pyramid "X" ing* (1965) is illustrated on p. 101 and *1,2,3 Check* (1965) on p. 102.

Schulze, Franz. *Fantastic Images: Chicago Art Since 1945,* Chicago, Follett Publishing Co., 1972.
In this major history of Postwar Chicago art, Schulze states that "'Chicago-type art' is not only not rational, it is anti-rational to the point of perversity. It does not at all cherish logic, or clarity, or the open, declamatory mode of artistic statement that characterizes Chicago building—or, for that matter, most post-World War II American painting. It tends rather toward highly personal, introverted and obsessive styles and those who create it are usually more doggedly infatuated with symbol, image, dream and pungent anecdote than they are concerned with the need to give these elements articulate form."

Following his introduction, Schulze includes Urry among 17 major Chicago artists and writes (p. 188) that there is "a heavy muscularity to [Urry's] rambling aluminum blooms and big color gobbets, and even a winking wit which seems to derive from comic strip sources. When he first exhibited in the Phalanx shows of the mid-1960s, his garrulously arrhythmic sculptures looked very much at home alongside the grimy styles of younger artists like Jim Nutt and Karl Wirsum. . . . If there is a difference between him and them, it is mostly in the scale and abstractness of his sculpture." Schulze traces this difference to the influence of San Francisco art on Urry.

Nine Urry sculptures—*Headscape* (1968), *Moon Ribbon* (1969), *Untitled* (1969), *Earth Mother* (1969), *Popeil Commission* (1971), *Psychedilly Rose* (1967), *Blat* (1967), *Oop-Zig* (1966), and *Round Series #6* (1966), pp. 189-197.

Riedy, James L. *Chicago Sculpture,* Urbana, University of Illinois Press, 1981. Describes (pp 150-152) *Resurrection,* Urry's sculpture which was mounted on the façade of the Elizabeth M. Cudahy Memorial Library on the Loyola University Chicago Lake Shore campus. According to the text, the sculpture "consists of two complementary forms" making "an autonomous work of art. One of the two fabricated aluminum structures is just in front of the building; its 25 ft. companion piece placed behind it crawls up the façade, beginning about 15 ft. above the ground. Together both pieces function as a unit in solving the problem that challenged the sculptor: 'I was trying to define space—to integrate the grounds with the building." A dispute resulted when Urry delivered a different design than promised and Loyola did not pay the full amount of the commission.

Andrews, Oliver. *Living Materials: A Sculptor's Handbook,* Berkeley, University of California Press, 1983. A photograph of *Psychedilly Rose* (1967) appears on p. 278. The caption reads: "Here we see casting used in an unusual way, to create linear rather than volumetric forms. The artist capitalizes on the ability of casting to make shapes that are flowing and organic."

Sinkevitch, Alice. *American Institute of Architects Guide to Chicago,* New York, Harcourt Brace & Company, 1993. Description on pp. 234-235 of the Loyola University Chicago Lake Shore Campus and Urry's sculpture which was mounted on the façade of the Elizabeth M. Cudahy Memorial Library. The sculpture, originally titled *Erection* and later rechristened *Resurrection,* is said to obscure the architectural design of the façade.

Zabriskie: Fifty Years, New York, Ruder Finn Press, 2004. History of the Virginia Zabriskie Gallery documents Urry's shows in 1969, 1972, and 1976. No photographs or text accompany.

Hidden Loyola. Loyola University Chicago Digital Special Collections, (www.lib.luc.edu/special collections), 2010. Online presentation based on Michael Grace, S.J.'s, yearly tour of architectural treasures at Loyola's Lake Shore campus includes a brief, illustrated account of Urry's *Resurrection* which was commissioned for the façade of the Elizabeth M. Cudahy Memorial Library.

Luecking, Steve. *John Henry,* New York, Ruder Finn Press, 2010, pp. 18-19, describes Urry's "contorted" use of space in his historical essay "Lines of Giants: The Sculpture of John Henry." In "Interview: John Henry Talks with David Finn" (p. 34), Henry calls Urry a "powerful influence," adding that "He knew no boundaries. There was a sense that anything he could dream up, he could build."

Robins, Anthony W. *The Hotel Albert 23 East 10th Street, NYC: A History*, Thompson & Columbus, Inc., April 2011. This history of a New York hotel lists writers and artists who stayed there. Steve Urry's 1968 visit is mentioned, quoting from Brian D. Boyer's 1968 *Chicago Tribune* article about SJU's Royal Marks Gallery exhibition. Book is available online: http://thehotelalbert.com/download/hotel_albert_history.pdf

Urry is listed in the following reference works:

AskART (database: http://askart.com/) the *Artist's Bluebook,* Scottsdale, Arizona, (began in 2007). Also see http://lccn.loc.gov/2003557423
Davenport's Art Reference & Price Guide, Phoenix, LTB Gordonsart Inc., 2008.
Dictionary of Contemporary American Artists, New York, St. Martins Press, 1982, 1988, and 1994 editions.
Who's Who in American Art; (Ed. Jacques Cattell Press), New York, St. R.R. Bowker, 1976.
Who's Who in America, Chicago, Marquis Who's Who, 1970-1971 and 1972-1973.
Who was Who in American Art 1564-1975: 400 Years of Artists in America, Madison, Connecticut, Sound View Press, 1999.

EDUCATION

School of the Art Institute of Chicago, 1957-1959. The school has no record of Urry, but he may have taken art classes without registering as a degree candidate.

University of Chicago, 1957-1959. The university has no record of Urry, but he may have taken art classes at the Midway Studios without registering as a degree candidate.

California College of Arts and Crafts, 1960-1961. Now called the California College of the Arts, this institution has no record of Urry, but witnesses remember him there. He met his future wife Tassy at the CCAC and she says that he took a watercolor class there. The fall semester ran from September 12, 1960 - January 24, 1961, and the spring semester from February 1 - June 8, 1961.

San Francisco Art Institute, 1961-1962. According to attendance and grade records, Urry took drawing and color (William Brown), sculpture (Jeremy Anderson), and metal sculpture (David Tolerton) in the fall semester, 1961. In the spring semester 1962, he took painting/studio (James Budd Dixon) and Eastern art history (Joseph Pugliese).

SAN FRANCISCO

Sculptures

Untitled (Gift to Father). 1961. Welded steel, 39½ x 6 x 5½ in.

Untitled (Gift to Mother). 1961. Welded steel, 18½ x 5¾ x 5½ in.

Untitled (Gift to Lynn). 1961. Welded steel, 12½ x 8½ x 11 in.

Works on Paper

Untitled (Sausalito). Inscribed "For Jan".1960. Watercolor, 17¼ x 23¼ in.

CHICAGO

Sculptures

Double X. 1965. Lacquered and welded steel, 83½ x 77 x 42¼ in. Collection of the Museum of Contemporary Art, Chicago. Gift of Jerry Peart. 1987.12.

Head Flower. 1967. Cast and welded aluminum, 108 x 48 x 16 in. Collection of Elmhurst College, Illinois.

Untitled (Claire Prussian's piece). Signed "S. Urry 69".Cast and welded aluminum, 21½ x 24½ x 25¾ in. Collection of Claire Prussian, Chicago.

Winged Thing. Signed "S. Urry 69".Purchased, October 16, 1969. Cut and welded aluminum, 30 x 15 x 9 in. Collection of Playboy Enterprises, Los Angeles.

From the *Popeil Chess Set.* 1970. Cast/formed aluminum, (Seven pieces in different shapes ranging from 2½ to 7½ in. high.) Collection of Pamela Popeil, Chicago.

Untitled (Ivory-colored sculpture). 1969. Signed "For Kay 1969." Cast and welded aluminum, ivory paint, 16½ x 12½ x 6¾ in. Collection of Kay Urry DeMarsche.

Untitled (Three fingers). Signed and dated "S. Urry 70".Cast aluminum, 7¾ x 8½ x 1¼ in. Collection of Janis Urry.

Untitled (Biomorphic forms). Signed "S. Urry 70".6¾ x 1¾ x 11 in. Collection of Janis Urry.

Untitled (Circular sculpture with cloud base). 1971. Cast and welded aluminum, 9¼ x 10½ in. Collection of the David and Alfred Smart Museum of Art, University of Chicago. Gift of Mrs. Marion Simon, 1985.99.

Loop and Spiral, NYC. 1971. Cast and welded aluminum, 40 x 70 x 42 in. Collection of Robert Bergman.

Untitled (Spiraling Up) Signed Urry "71" with circled numeral 9 (etched into base). Cut, welded, formed aluminum 8½ x 12 x 8¾ in. Collection of Barbara and Erwin Glass.

Untitled (Open arch over column topped by cloud form). Signed "Urry 71" with circled number 7 (etched into base). Cut, welded, formed aluminum 16½ x 13 x 14½ in. Collection of Barbara and Erwin Glass.

Arch. Signed "Urry 1972" (etched into base). Cast bronze, 15 x 5 x 5 in., David and Alfred Smart Museum of Art, University of Chicago, Chicago. The Joseph P. Shure Collection, 2010.181.

Untitled (Gift to parents). Signed "S. Urry 72" (inscribed to parents). Pale green cast Lucite, 18 x 6½ x 1¾ in. Collection of Janis Urry.

Untitled (Gift to Lynn). Signed "S. Urry 72 for Lynn".Cast Lucite, 8 x 4¾ x 3 in. Collection of Lynn Urry.

Waxes

Untitled Waxes (Arch). 1970s. Black wax, 11 x 4¾ x 3 in.; (leaning arch). 1970s. Black wax, 14 x 10½ x 2½ in. Collection of the Sedgwick Studio.

Works on Paper

Untitled (manipulated Polaroid photograph of industrial scene). Early 1970s. 10 x 10 in. Collection of Janis Urry.

NEW YORK

Sculptures

Untitled (Reclining Figure). Ca. 1973. Sawed aluminum, 3 x 17 x 8½ in. Collection of Mary Ann Keeler, Grand Rapids, Michigan.

Untitled (O-shape and long S-shape). Signed and dated "S. Urry 1973". Sawed aluminum S-Form, 12¼ x 6 x 3 in.; O-Form. 10 x 6¼ x 2¼. Collection of Dawn Clark Netsch, Chicago.

Untitled (Seven-part puzzle piece). Signed "summer 1975". Sawed aluminum, 35½ in. circumference when assembled. Collection of the Grand Rapids Art Museum. Gift of an Anonymous Donor, 1978.41.

Untitled (Cloud). Signed and dated "S. Urry 1973". Sawed aluminum, 14¼ x 8⅝ x 3 in. Collection of the Grand Rapids Art Museum, Michigan. Gift of Conrad and Molly Bradshaw, 2004.17.

Untitled. Ca. 1976. Sawed aluminum, 9¾ x 14½ in. Collection of the Muskegon Museum of Art, Muskegon, MI. Hackley Picture Fund purchase, 1977.2.

Untitled (Double Starburst Piece, Small Starburst inside Large). Ca. 1980s. Sawed aluminum, 7¾ x 9 x 3½ in. Collection of John Adduci.

Untitled (For John). Signed "Urry 82" 1982. Three-piece cast and sawed aluminum sculpture whose elements fit together. Lightning bolt shape, 4¼ x 2 x 1¼ in; Small cast arch 6½ x 2¼ x 1¼ in; Flat-topped sawed arch, 6½ x 2½ x 2 in. Collection of John Adduci.

Untitled (Cut piece with multiple holes and steel balls). Ca. 1982. Cast/welded/sawed aluminum, steel, 12½ x 8 x 6¾ in. Collection of John Adduci.

Untitled (Inset starburst and long cast form arching over top). Ca. 1982. Cast and welded, sawed aluminum, 21 x 23 x 2¾ in. Collection of Janis Urry.

Untitled (Three-piece sculpture with flat plate, block, and constructed tunnel form). Ca. 1982. Cast and welded, sawed aluminum, 11¾ x 8 x 8¾ in. Outer portion: 8¼ x 9 x 3¾ in; inner portion: 4¼ x 6½ x 3¼ in. Collection of Janis Urry.

Untitled (Dan's Puzzle Piece). Ca. 1982. Sawed aluminum, 16 x 4¼ x 3 in. (Work not completed). Collection of Dan Blue.

Untitled (Three-part piece with pins and holes. At left are two stacked semicircles; middle is two-walled piece with tops joined, large hole in center; right is three finger-like forms.) Ca. 1980s. Cut, formed aluminum, 7½ x 9½ x 9 in. Collection of Dan Blue.

Untitled (Painted piece with long horizontal extension, bowl welded on). ca. 1985. Formed and welded aluminum; oil paint, automotive spray paint 20½ x 18½ x 10 in. Collection of John Adduci.

Untitled (Painted piece with orange Z at center). Ca. 1985. Formed and welded aluminum, oil paint, automotive spray paint, 15½ x 19½ x 10½ in. Collection of John Adduci.

Untitled (Painted piece leaning sharply to left, inverted dome at top left). Ca. 1985. Formed and welded aluminum, oil paint, automotive spray paint, 24½ x 30 x 15 in. Collection of John Adduci.

Drawings

Untitled drawing of knotted sculpture. Signed "Urry 76". 14 x 11 in.

Untitled preparatory drawing for polyurethane isocyanate resin sculpture. Signed "Urry 76" Pencil on paper, 11 x 14 in.

Untitled drawing of arch sculpture. Signed "S. Urry 76." Pencil on paper, 13 x 10½ in. Collection of S. Thomas Scarff.